The Promise

The Promise

GOD'S ANSWER WAS NOT MINE, BUT WAS MORE THAN ENOUGH

Karen Easter

REVIEW AND HERALD® PUBLISHING ASSOCIATION
HAGERSTOWN, MD 21741-1119

The author assumes full responsibility for the accuracy of all facts and quotations as cited
in this book.

This book was
Edited by Gerald Wheeler
Designed by Tina M. Ivany
Cover photo by PictureQuest
Electronic makeup by Shirley M. Bolivar
Typeset: Bembo 11/15

PRINTED IN U.S.A.

10 09 08 07 06   5 4 3 2 1

R&H Cataloging Service
Easter, Karen
    The promise.

        1. Adoption—   2. Abortion.   I. Title.

                        362.7086945

ISBN 978-0-8280-1886-9

DEDICATION

To the many single women
who are experiencing the challenges and decisions
that result from an unplanned pregnancy.
Once you begin this journey, none of the choices you make
will be physically and/or emotionally pain free.
I challenge you to seek God's will.
He will journey with you and provide comfort and guidance
through every step of the way
as He leads you into a brighter tomorrow.

ACKNOWLEDGMENTS

There are several people who played a key role in the writing of this book. For their inspiration, guidance, and faith, I will be forever grateful.

First, I'd like to thank the "Wheeler Trilogy"—Robyn, your tutoring and brainstorming with me each week, while eating Dunkin Donuts, was an incredible gift. You taught me so much about writing. Penny, your interest, faith, and support of this project from Day One inspired me to keep writing. And Gerald, you did an awesome job at polishing and editing this manuscript.

And Jeannette, thanks for your many words of encouragement and for your willingness to acknowledge the "elephant in the living room" and to publish this story.

Special thanks to Emily, who made these characters come alive; and Tony, for working with me in the writing lab.

Thanks to my beautiful daughters, who make me so proud, and to my husband, who loves me unconditionally and encourages and supports my passion for writing. You are more than I ever could have wished for.

Prologue: Week 10

PROLOGUE: WEEK 10

Faint light filtered through the mini-blinds covering the bathroom window that Sunday morning as Karen fumbled with the small container. The plastic crinkled as she unwrapped the box and cautiously removed its contents. Squinting at the small print on the paper insert, she struggled to wake up enough to follow the instructions properly.

Peering into the mirror, her sleepy eyes—almost hidden under her tousled shoulder-length dark hair—looked back at her with fear. *What if . . . ?* Her breath caught in her throat. *Stop it,* she told herself, hands shaking.

After completing the task and setting a timer for three minutes, she walked to the kitchen and poured herself a glass of orange juice. Her mind raced while she paced restlessly, her purple silk pajamas swishing as she walked back and forth.

During the past few weeks Karen had been feeling sluggish: nothing specific, just not herself. She had the right to feel a bit under the weather, she rationalized, since she'd been through so many stresses within the past year. Her husband had divorced her after 18 years of marriage. Then came the move to conservative New England from Colorado and a new job as the guidance counselor at a Christian high school. And in September her 17-year-old daughter, Sarah, had left for a year in Europe as a foreign exchange student. No wonder the emotional roller coaster that had been the past year of her life had left her feeling drained.

The timer beeped and Karen shuffled back to the bathroom, reassuring herself that she had nothing to worry about. *I'm fine. No big deal.* She stopped at the bathroom door. It was the moment of truth, something that might change the course of her life forever. Then she caught herself. Of course, that was foolish. Melodramatic, she told herself. Such things didn't happen to mature—to Christian—women. Still she hesitated, frozen, one hand on the doorknob.

This is crazy!

Taking a deep breath, she walked through the doorway. Then, dazed and bewildered, she stared at the pregnancy test. *No. No. NO!*

The room started to spin and her legs gave out. Sinking onto the hard floor, she leaned against the sink, head pounding, heart racing. She struggled to breathe, her panic-stricken body forgetting its normal functions. Tears flowed down her face as reality ricocheted through her mind. *How could I be pregnant?* she asked herself again and again. Her stomach knotted, and she felt herself about to throw up. Holding herself tightly, she crawled toward the toilet. The nausea passed, but her body shook uncontrollably.

Grabbing the pregnancy test off the counter, she hurled it against the wall. *No, God. Please, no! God, I promise, if You let this be a mistake. . . .*

At the drugstore, hurried and embarrassed, she'd accidentally grabbed a box containing two tests, and now she felt grateful that she had. Frantically, she tore open the other package and started the second test, certain that the first one was an error.

Now she waited, counting the minutes, pacing back and forth outside the bathroom door, praying furiously. *God, I promise I'll do anything if You'll just—* Thoughts of herself donating her entire month's paycheck to her church's building fund as a bribe flitted through her mind. Three minutes had never seemed so long. Again the timer rang. Again she went through the bathroom door. And again—the same result.

She hardly knew that she stumbled back to bed, crawling in between crisp, flowery sheets. Burying her face in the pillow, she sobbed uncontrollably.

It's a bad dream, only a dream. I'll wake up and begin my day again. She remembered the nightmares that she had had when she was a child— dreams of monsters chasing her around a large house in which every door she opened led to nothing. Even now she could remember the panic she had felt then, even in her sleep, and the intensity of the relief she experienced when she would wake up safe in her bed. Desperately she longed for that same relief now—for a way out. When she pinched herself the hard, sharp pain did not wake her up, and the sobs burst forth again.

What will I tell my family? How will I explain this to Sarah? How will I survive financially without a job? Do I want to start over and raise a child at my age? Should I have an abortion and pretend that this never happened? On and on the questions came, as relentless and frightening as the monsters of her childhood nightmares.

I have to pull myself together and think of a solution. A person who prided herself on being organized and resourceful, Karen was unaccustomed to feeling helpless. *I'll think of something,* she repeated. *One step at a time. First, get out of bed.* Forcing herself to get up, she slipped on her robe and walked to the living room where she stared out the big picture window. *Everything is so bleak this time of year,* she thought, missing the summertime green of the sprawling lawn in front of her apartment. The overcast sky offered no hope of sunshine. Even the trees, gray and bare after shedding their leaves for the season, seemed sad and forlorn. Gazing at a large tree not far from the window, Karen noticed a single leaf hanging from an otherwise naked branch. Suddenly a gust of wind ripped the leaf from the branch. It swirled to the ground and skidded across the lawn.

I'm supposed to be a role model at a Christian school, and here I am in this situation. Just last week Rachel, a senior, had sat sobbing in Karen's small office, pouring out her concerns about her boyfriend wanting more from her than she thought was right. Karen had hugged her and shared words of encouragement. "Don't give in. Tell him you can't be pressured. It's worth the wait." The following day the girl was smiling again and had thanked her. *What will she think of me when this scandal hits?* Karen wondered, feeling like such a hypocrite.

And this is certain to be a scandal. If I just disappear, that would raise a lot of questions, but if I stay, then everyone will find out, and I'll get fired. The feeling of panic rose in her again. *Stop,* she told herself. *Stop thinking about it. Face the day. One step at a time, remember? Shower. I need to take a shower.*

Like a robot she headed for the bathroom. Slipping off her clothes, she stepped into the shower. *Perhaps this will soothe my nerves,* she hoped as she twisted the chrome knobs, making the water as hot as she could stand it. As the water poured down on her, she tried to find some solution. But nothing seemed workable. *Think of something else. The book I'm reading—think about that.* But it didn't help. Finally she dried herself off and went back to bed. As she lay on her pillow she absent-mindedly traced the marks left from her earlier tears. *God, please—* She tried to form a prayer, but words wouldn't come. Then she began to sob so hard her eyes throbbed. Eventually she ran out of tears and simply lay there with puffy red eyes. *What am I going to do?* she asked herself for the umpteenth time that day.

Overwhelmed with the implications of how this would affect her and the Christian community in which she worked and lived, she suddenly felt the need to immerse herself in what was most familiar—music. Hurrying to the living room, she grabbed the first CD she could find. As her fingers opened the case, she glanced down at the cover and came face to face with a photo of Rick, the father of her baby, and gasped out loud.

She had been so caught up in her own shock and fear that she hadn't stopped to consider him and how it would affect his life. What would the pregnancy do to a ministry that he had spent his entire life building?

THREE YEARS EARLIER

The sun glistened off Karen's deep-blue Volvo as she drove through the stone gates of the music festival grounds in Estes Park, Colorado, that Monday morning. Spectacular beds of flowers, ranging from bright yellows to bold purples, outlined the winding paved road leading up to the pavilion. Sprinklers rotated rhythmically, watering the meticulously manicured gardens.

As she pulled into the large parking lot, she glanced at a mammoth wooden lodge nestled to the right of the pavilion and wondered if that was where the guests would stay. Curious to see how many people would attend the competition and eagerly anticipating working with other professionals within the Christian music industry, she went inside and joined the registration line.

The event's sponsors had chosen her, a moderately established songwriter, as one of seven judges for the weeklong annual music competition hosted for new Christian artists. Although several well-known singers had recorded her songs and she occasionally received royalty checks, she still considered it only a hobby. She had finally completed college and now enjoyed her work as a guidance counselor.

As the line moved slowly she glanced down at the packet of information she'd received. It was a prestigious competition, offering the winners in each category recording contracts with the finest Christian record companies. Required to register by 11:00 a.m., the judges had to attend an afternoon orientation before the opening ceremonies scheduled to begin at 7:00. Subsequent evenings would feature competitions in all music categories, including soloists, groups, and instrumentalists. The final awards would be presented Saturday night at the conclusion of the competition.

The organizers of the convention treated the judges to a light lunch in an adjacent room following registration. The president of the Gospel Music Association, Gavin McAllister, a tall heavyset man in his mid-fifties with well-trimmed auburn hair and a mustache, made formal introductions. As he listed each name and read a short summary of their area of expertise and accomplishments, the judge would stand in acknowledgment. Karen knew many of the other judges by sight. The last person to be introduced was Rick Davidson, and she recognized him immediately. Following the introductions, everyone milled around, making new acquaintances and renewing old friendships.

Rick had recorded many CDs. "Pleased to meet you," he said as he approached Karen and extended his hand. "I'm familiar with a couple of your songs, and I like your writing style."

A little taken aback at his deep voice and open smile, she managed to reply, "Thank you. I admire your music also." As they shook hands she noticed that he seemed to be giving her his full attention. He dressed with impeccable taste, his clothes accentuating his tall frame, and he carried himself in a confident manner.

Following orientation, Rick caught up with her in the cafeteria. "Mind if I join you?" he inquired.

"Sure, I'd enjoy the company." She set her tray on a corner table, and he chose a seat directly across from her.

After placing her napkin in her lap, Karen gazed around the cafeteria. The massive windows with their full-length gold and green lined draperies welcomed the sunshine into the room, and large golden chandeliers, dangling from the high ceiling, provided additional light. Large Picasso and Monet prints accented by heavy gold frames graced the walls, and soft classical music played on the built-in sound system.

In between bites of spaghetti they chatted. "Tell me, where do you live, and what's your family like?" he asked, glancing at her wedding ring.

"I live in a small town a couple hours from here," she began, wiping her mouth with her napkin. "I'm married and have a daughter. Sarah's 14 going on 20." She smiled as she pictured Sarah—tall for her age, blond, with a relaxed attitude about life. "Anyway, my 'day-job' is at a local Christian school where I'm a guidance counselor—I advise students with their career choices and also handle scholastic testing. But my creative outlet and real passion is music." After sipping her drink, she asked, "How about you?" wondering what he was really like.

"My address is on the East Coast. However, I spend most of my time on the road," he said. "I perform more than 150 concerts a year, so I'm gone every weekend, touring. From time to time I take a break and produce albums for other artists."

"Oh? Tell me more about producing! That's always intrigued me." Breaking off a corner of her garlic bread, Karen began playing with it.

"Producing is my 'creative outlet,' as you called it. Concerts can become routine and boring if you're not careful. Producing is much more creative and something that I'd like to pursue full-time eventually." He leaned back in his chair, and she noticed a gleam in his eye as he spoke. "I love starting with a simple concept and musical arrangements that only I can imagine and then turning them into a finished recording project. For now I'm comfortable with life on the road, but some day I'll tire of it."

Karen listened intently, wishing he would share more. "Ever been married?" she asked.

"Yes, I got married in my 20s, and the marriage lasted eight years." With his fork he toyed with two remaining strands of spaghetti. "Eventually the stresses of life on the road got to be too much for my wife, so she left and took our child." Sadness echoed in his voice, and he quickly changed the subject.

"When I was growing up my family was very involved in music," he said, "and my dad taught me to play the guitar and to harmonize. Although I spent a couple years in college, my heart wasn't in it. Eventually I went into full-time music ministry."

Glancing at his watch, he then took her empty tray and added it to his. "We'd better hurry, or we'll be late for the opening competition."

That week they spent much of their time together. In addition to sharing meals, they would sit on the large wooden porch of the lodge every evening and chat about the competition, discuss well-known artists within the industry, and share ideas about songwriting.

During supper on Thursday evening their conversation wandered onto the subject of Karen's marriage. "Are you happily married?" he inquired.

Caught off guard, she paused, fiddling with her fork. "That's a difficult question. I guess I'm not sure what happiness is anymore," she began, enjoying having someone to talk with who paid attention to everything she said. "When we got married we were both very different people. We never had any common interests, so I don't know what brought us together." She stared out the nearby window, watching the pine trees swaying freely in the breeze. "Sometimes I wonder . . ." she began, but caught herself and left the thought unfinished.

"A marriage takes a lot of hard work," he said eventually. "If you can make it work, for Sarah's sake, it'd be the best thing. Separation is very difficult." Karen knew that he was right.

Although the culmination of the week's events was the award ceremony Saturday evening, Sunday brunch was the last planned activity for all participants and judges. Over a meal of pancakes, Danishes, fried potatoes, and a multitude of fresh fruit, Rick and Karen enjoyed one last leisurely conversation before making their way to the parking lot with their bags.

"I guess this is it," he began as he glanced down at the business card that she had given him earlier when he had requested her phone number. "Let's keep in touch, and perhaps we can get together sometime and do some songwriting."

She agreed with a smile.

TWO YEARS LATER

True to their promise, they had kept in touch sporadically during the next couple years. Each lengthy conversation had focused on their shared passion for music—what was new in the industry, his concert tours, and the latest song that she was writing.

When her husband filed for divorce, Rick was one of the first people that she told, and just possibly, deep inside where she wouldn't acknowledge it, she thought, *Maybe Rick and I . . .* He provided encouragement when she needed someone to talk with and gave her advice about accepting the position as guidance counselor at the school in New England. It would be, he stressed, an excellent opportunity for her to make a fresh start in a new and beautiful part of the country. Without fully realizing what was happening, she began to depend on him, looking forward to their conversations and his advice. He always knew what to do. At his urging she took the job in New England.

The new school would be different than the one in Colorado. Since it was a boarding institution instead of a day school, Karen would have responsibilities in addition to counseling and scholastic testing. However, there would also be fewer students—only about 100 instead of the 300 that she was used to—so there was the potential to become acquainted with them on a more personal level. That idea appealed to her—she had always considered her career a ministry in which she could help, encourage, and befriend students.

After Karen had settled into her new job, she and Rick had their first date.

"Trust me," he said with a big smile each time she begged for details. Rick arrived at her apartment that spring evening dressed in casual navy pants and a starched button-up blue-and-white dress shirt. His dark hair was combed perfectly, and he smelled of expensive cologne. Karen felt both attracted to him and nervous at the same time. She thought back to high school and the boys she had dated then. And all these years she had been thinking that she'd never feel butterflies in her stomach again! As they walked out of her apartment, Karen quickly glanced at the mirror by the door. *Do I look OK?* She had forgotten how nerve-wracking first dates were!

Always the gentleman, Rick opened the car door for her, and they drove to his favorite restaurant. The parking lot was full outside the beige stucco building. Karen's heart sank as she wondered how long the wait would be. *At least I'm with Rick—that alone should make the time pass quickly.* Once inside they encountered almost 20 people mingling around, waiting for tables to become available. Rick smiled graciously at the hostess and pulled her aside, whispering something that Karen couldn't hear. Immediately a waitress appeared and guided them to a quiet corner table, lighting the candle in the center.

Stunned, Karen looked questioningly at Rick, who nonchalantly glanced at his menu with a subtle grin. *I wonder what other tricks he has up his sleeve?* Resisting the urge to reach across the table and grab his hand, she concentrated on her menu instead. *Calm down—don't fall for him so fast!*

Despite her caution, Karen still savored each moment when he gazed into her eyes during the meal. Conversation came easy and encompassed a wide range of topics. *I haven't had this much fun in a long time,* she thought with a twinge of wistfulness. *Maybe Rick and I . . . .* She pushed away thoughts of the future. *It's just one date. There's no guarantee there'll be others . . .* As they finished the chocolate brownie sundae that they were sharing, he glanced at his watch and suggested that they hurry so they would get to their next stop on time. Intrigued, she played along.

They drove downtown to a large theater where the billboard listed a famous jazz musician as being the artist of the evening. People streamed through the double doors with great anticipation. She smiled at Rick. *How did he know?* He took her hand during the concert, and she felt content. *We do have a future together!* The thought hit her during the last song. She was sure of it.

Their phone calls grew in frequency and length as they shared their daily activities and their thoughts with each other. During one conversation he excitedly explained that he had just been asked to produce an album for a new Christian artist who lived within a half-hour of Karen's apartment. He would be in the area for four months during the recording of the album.

The first six weeks that Rick was in town flew by, and he spent almost every evening at her apartment. Quickly making himself at home, he offered to prepare many of the meals, explaining that he rarely had the opportunity to cook while traveling. Always with a flair for detail, he prepared a wide variety of delicacies: stroganoff served with salad. Fresh corn-on-the-cob from a nearby farm with burgers and all of the toppings. Three-egg cheese omelets with mushrooms, green peppers, and black olives. Dessert always included some form of chocolate, from berry ice cream dripping in chocolate sauce and peanuts, to rich layer cakes.

During each meal they discussed the progress of the recording sessions, enjoying their friendship that continued to develop.

Occasionally on weekends they took day trips to various scenic attractions around the state. In the car they listened to their favorite music and discussed their lives. It always surprised them how similar their backgrounds and beliefs were. *We're so perfect together.* The thought reoccurred more and more frequently as she and Rick grew closer.

One evening while sitting on the couch watching television he took her hand and cautiously asked, "When will your divorce be final?"

"Soon." Her heart raced. "Why?" she asked shyly, feeling like an awkward teenager.

"Because I want to be more than friends," he admitted, bending toward her to kiss her tenderly.

Their relationship blossomed more and more as they spent most of their time together. However, the constant togetherness brought new challenges—challenges that reminded them just how human Christians really are. Once they had transitioned from friendship to dating, they realized that they would have to set boundaries to the intimacy of their relationship.

"Karen," he began, turning off the television as they sat on the couch one evening. "We really need to talk about the temptations that we've been struggling with." He fidgeted as he looked at her. "We've come pretty close to—" he began, unsure how to phrase what had been going through his mind. "I want to stay committed to God and to my ministry, and you have important commitments, too. Somehow we have to find a way to stay strong and remain pure—honoring God's plan for our lives." He paused, taking her hand.

"I agree," she blushed. "I would never want to disappoint God—or the students that I work with, either." Sighing, she laid her head on his shoulder, enjoying the lingering scent of his cologne. "But you've gotta quit wearing this stuff," she teased, playfully slapping him on the arm as she sat up straight.

"OK, I'll cut down on the cologne," he chuckled. "But seriously, we need to avoid situations that we know will be a problem. I need to go home earlier each evening, for one thing." He sighed as he looked into her eyes. "This isn't going to be easy."

It wasn't.

• • • •

One Sunday evening Rick and Karen attended an outdoor Southern gospel festival in the foothills of Pennsylvania. They had coordinated the trip to coincide with two concerts that he had performed at a nearby city that weekend.

The trees had turned brilliant shades of red, orange, and yellow, heralding the fall season. After driving down a long, narrow, winding back road, they pulled into the large grassy parking area. As they stepped from his gray sedan, she stretched, inhaling the crisp mountain air. Looking skyward, she watched the fluffy white clouds floating effortlessly through the bright-blue sky.

Hand in hand, they sauntered slowly toward the outdoor amphitheater. Apparently it had been there for years, for its wood, although painted white, was peeling and worn. The stage was nothing fancy, just a simple structure that rose four feet above the ground. It was the only portion covered by a roof. A backdrop had one door on each side, providing easy access to dressing areas backstage.

An odd mixture of seats formed not quite perfect rows in front of the stage. One section consisted of wooden benches in various shades of weather-beaten gray. Another area included folding metal chairs ranging from silver to dark gray, with an occasional tan chair interspersed. The regular attendees—the hard-core fans—were easy to spot. They had brought more comfortable lawn chairs. To them, the monthly concerts were spiritual gatherings, and they faithfully attended each and every one.

The open-air amphitheater nestled in a picturesque valley surrounded by rolling hills on all sides. Shortly after the concert began, the sun slowly sank beyond the horizon, and the tall pine trees covering the hillside turned a deep purple.

For nearly three hours Rick and Karen sat, stood, clapped, smiled, and savored the moments—moments full of music, their shared passion—moments that bonded them, drawing them even closer. Many times throughout the concert they had turned toward each other at the same instant, responding with similar comments or facial expressions. Their thoughts were identical, their reactions and responses so intimate. Several times they stared in wonder at each other, as if to say, "You always seem to know what I'm thinking!"

After the concert they each bubbled with excitement. Although it was late, and they would have to travel several hours before they would reach their destination, they had stayed until the very last song. And the magic and wonder of the evening continued throughout their journey home. Somehow, enveloped in the afterglow of the concert, it was as if they were young again—laughing, talking, flirting, full of wonder, like children on Christmas morning. Being together felt so right. It seemed that they were meant for each other.

Arriving at their destination, he walked her toward the door, his arm around her, pulling her close as if to make sure the moment would never end. The air was cool and crisp. Stars spangled the black sky like diamonds splashed carelessly across velvet. Once inside they embraced, continuing to bask in the intimacy they felt at the concert. Without a word, he gazed into her eyes for an instant that seemed more like a lifetime, the oneness consuming them.

Where is this going? She felt herself slipping deeper into the moment. *Don't!* a small voice whispered in her head. It had spoken to her many times before. Both she and Rick had made a commitment a few months before, and so far they had managed to resist the increasing temptation.

He reached down and pulled her chin toward him, kissing her tenderly.

Go now, while you still can. The voice grew more intense. And so did their desire to be together. The evening had been so magical that neither one wanted it to end.

But by morning the magic had turned into guilt and shame.

WEEK 10

How am I going to tell Rick? Karen had lost track of how many times she had asked herself that question. It had been less than four hours since she had discovered that she was thirtysomething, divorced, and pregnant. Finally getting dressed, as she snapped her jeans she absent-mindedly thought, *I wonder how much longer I'll be able to wear these?* Her mind flashed back to when she had been pregnant with Sarah, and she remembered that she hadn't shown much until the very end. *OK, I can hide this for a while,* she consoled herself. *But I have to tell Rick right away.* She needed to share her burden with someone.

I wish Rick were here so that I didn't have to tell him this over the phone, she thought as she paced around the living room. On one side of it sat an over-stuffed green and mauve couch nestled between a set of matching antique wood end tables. Each dark cherry stand had one small drawer and Queen Anne's legs. She had discovered them at a little antique shop while killing time on a recent trip. Across from the couch, taking up most of one wall, was a mahogany entertainment center that housed a large color television set and a modern stereo through which she had her television wired to enhance its sound. On each end of the entertainment unit stood built-in bookshelves holding a few special books and knickknacks. But she was oblivious to everything around her now.

Her stomach was in knots, and her heart pounded as she continued to wonder how to break the news to Rick. *What will he say?* A wave of nausea engulfed her body, and she ran for the bathroom. *My nerves can't handle this.* She sat on the cold tile floor, unable to throw up.

Rick was in Virginia performing that weekend and had called late the evening before to report on how the Saturday evening concert had gone. It was part of his unwinding process following each performance. As he spoke about the audience reaction, as well as any mistakes that he might have made, he would begin to relax. Karen had attended many weekend concerts with him and missed being with him to hear his updates in person.

Well, here goes nothing, she mused, picking up the white cordless phone and punching his cell phone number as she sat down on the couch.

A deep voice answered. Instantly an image of his handsome face flashed through her mind, allowing her to smile for a second before the reason for her call snapped her back to reality.

Her voice quivered as she squeaked out a barely audible, "Hi, there." Jumping to her feet, she resumed pacing.

After a pause he asked, "Is that you, Karen? I can hardly hear you."

Somehow she regained her composure. "How'd your concert go this morning?" Without thinking she started straightening knickknacks on the nearby bookshelf. At least she had control over them. It gave her an odd sense of strength.

"Excellent! The church was full, and the people responded well." He paused again. "I'm eating lunch with the pastor and a few others right now."

"Oh!" It caught her off guard. "I won't keep you then. I'll call again this evening."

All that morning she had struggled with what to say to him. She had run through the scenario a dozen different times and in a dozen different ways, and none were comforting. He was older than she was and lived an independent life. Throughout their many conversations she had heard him acknowledge more than once that he had become accustomed to that independence. Plus, he was set in his ways after living alone for years. *What impact would a baby have on his perfect world?* she wondered, another knot forming in her stomach. *Is marriage a possibility?* Even from the beginning of their relationship she had hoped it would happen.

Another reason for her apprehension involved his uneasiness around children. On the rare occasions that he had spent time with Sarah he seemed on edge, unsure of how to relate to the girl. Part of the discomfort, Karen imagined, came from having been separated from his own child for so many years. She surmised it was a combination of lack of experience and a fear of becoming emotionally attached, thus allowing the possibility of being hurt again.

Whatever it was, it didn't take a rocket scientist to guess what his reaction would be to her news. Another wave of nausea engulfed her as she thought about the conversation.

Less than an hour later her phone rang. "Hey, something's wrong, what's the matter?" he asked in a worried tone. "I snuck out of my meeting so that I could call you back."

When she heard his voice the floodgates opened and the tears streamed down her flushed cheeks. Sitting in the mauve chair in her bedroom, her right arm around her legs that she had pulled up against her chest as she clung to the phone with her left hand, she thought, *If only he could be here, it wouldn't be so frightening . . .*

He spoke softly, wanting to comfort her. "Whatever it is can't be that bad. Tell me what's wrong." Then he waited patiently.

Her rehearsed speech was no longer on the tip of her tongue. Panicked, she wasn't sure how to begin. "I haven't felt well for a while," she managed to get out between sobs, wiping her eyes with the sleeve of her navy sweater. "I finally found out why." She struggled with the words. "I'm pregnant."

The only sound from the other end of the phone was something between a deep sigh and a moan. His silence tore at her. She wished he'd say something—anything! "Are you sure?" was all he could eventually muster.

"Yes." More sobs rocked her body as she hugged herself tighter.

After another long, agonizing pause he continued, "We tried so hard to wait—resisting time and time again—and we sincerely regretted that one mistake." Karen remembered how terrible they had both felt, and how they had prayed together for forgiveness, committing to try even harder in the future.

"I know," she acknowledged, tears streaming down her face and onto her sweater.

"Are you *really* sure?" he asked, bewilderment in his words.

"Yes; I took two tests." She now lapsed into silence.

His voice changed to a tone that she had never heard before. He remained unusually calm, but she sensed the terror filtering through.

"Well, raising a child isn't an option for either of us," he started nervously. "That isn't what you have in mind, is it?"

"I just found out this morning, Rick, and I'm still in shock. I don't know what to think." *That wasn't exactly what I had hoped to hear from you!*

"Wow, this is a lot to comprehend."

"I know." *Say something!* she wanted to shout at him. *Tell me what to do!*

Again he sighed. "I need to get back to this meeting." After an uncomfortable pause, he mumbled despondently, "How can I go back in there with a smile on my face and pretend that everything's all right?"

"I'm sorry. I should have waited until you got home to tell you." *Like it's easy for me!* she wanted to lash out, but bit her tongue instead.

"I'll call you tonight, and we'll talk more. We'll figure something out, I promise."

After saying goodbye, Karen felt emotionally drained by the fear in his voice. He had always been so self-confident and in control. Fear in him was a totally new emotion. *How can this be happening?* Her mind was awhirl. *God, why did You allow this to happen?* she shouted in her mind, anger sweeping over her. *We're good people! Yes, we had a moment of weakness, but do we really deserve this? Do something!* She punched a pillow lying on the couch, feeling the tears welling up.

Exhausted, she walked slowly, hesitantly, to the living room and over to the large mahogany bookcase. There in the center was a picture of Sarah, smiling back at her. As tears rolled down her cheeks, Karen spoke aloud to her daughter.

"Oh, Sarah," she sobbed. "How will I ever explain this to you?"

Shame swept over her. "After all the years I've tried to teach you to be pure, to wait until marriage for intimacy, what will you think of me now?" She wiped her eyes but the torrent of tears persisted. "I don't want you to find out that I've made mistakes. I wouldn't even know where to begin. . . ." Consumed by guilt, she laid her daughter's photograph face down on the shelf and headed toward the back door.

Grabbing her coat, she got into her car and drove toward a nearby waterfall, a place that she had discovered several months earlier and had escaped to whenever she needed to be alone. Music was her solace in times like this, and she slipped a Christian CD into the player. As the music soothed her, she prayed out loud. "Dear Father, we've made such a big mistake, and we don't know what to do. I need Your wisdom and grace more than ever. Please give Rick peace and forgiveness also. Please help me to trust in You, that You'll work something out." After a bit she felt a sense of peace. Somehow, she sensed, a solution would come.

Pulling onto the small dirt road that led the quarter of a mile back to the waterfall, she hoped that there wouldn't be anyone else there today. On hot summer afternoons she often encountered people wandering through the area but since it was a chilly fall day she surmised that she'd be the only visitor.

Sure enough, she had the place to herself. The dirt road ended near the foot of the 15-foot waterfall. A slow, steady stream of water poured down the cliff, and it looked exceptionally cold. She zipped her blue windbreaker as she wandered to a nearby wooden bench where she could sit and think.

What am I going to do? Her mind raced and her heart fluttered. *If I decide to keep the baby, I know I'll lose my job . . . Even if Rick and I get married, I'm sure I'll still lose my job . . . And getting another job, although I'm qualified, would be difficult once I've been fired.* Picking up a stone, she hurled it as hard as she could into the water. Fear petrified her. *I wonder if I could go through with an abortion?* Glancing up at the gray sky, she thought, *It seems the easiest way out. God, are You up there? I sure could use some practical advice right now.* Now she found herself wishing, as she had done when she was young and first learning the stories of the Bible, that God would come and sit down beside her and talk, face to face. "You feel so far away," she whispered, looking up at the sky. *I feel so alone.*

Karen continued to think and pray as she got up and began restlessly walking, kicking stones as she went. It was a chilly day, and she had to keep moving to keep warm. *Dear God, this is so horrible.* Tears streamed from her bloodshot eyes and down her pale cheeks. *I need peace and some answers. What am I going to do?*

As she gazed toward the sky once more, part of a text flashed through her mind. "Be anxious for nothing . . . the peace of God, which surpasses all understanding, will be with you." *Thank You, Lord, for that reassurance,* she prayed as a ray of hope filtered in. *It's not exactly an answer, but it's something to hold onto. And I could use anything right now.*

Eventually she retraced her steps to her car and headed for home. The drive was soothing, and she arrived at the apartment just as the sun was setting, feeling surprisingly more at peace.

As Karen unlocked her apartment, she heard a familiar voice call her name. Turning, she saw Emily strolling down the sidewalk carrying a bag of groceries. Tall, with an average build, the younger woman had shoulder-length brown hair. She was dressed in her usual—jeans and a 1980s-style blouse.

"Oh, hi! Where are your kids?" Karen asked, fumbling for words. She hoped her eyes were no longer bloodshot. Emily and her husband, Grant, had four children, all under the age of 7. The husband taught at the school where Karen worked, and Emily was a stay-at-home mom.

"Grant's watching them for a couple hours while I have a break and get some errands done." Before Karen could respond, Emily continued, "Why don't you stop by this evening? Come hang out a while."

"OK, I'll be by later." As soon as the words left her mouth, Karen regretted them. Normally she would enjoy getting out for an hour or two, relaxing with friends. But she was so preoccupied with her problem that she feared she'd break down in front of them. And although part of her wanted someone to confide in, Karen knew it was imperative that Grant and Emily not find out her secret. Not only was he an employee of the school, but he and Emily had never really liked Rick, believing that he would end up hurting Karen, and Grant had encouraged her to be careful in her relationship with him. She was in no mood to hear an "I told you so." Still feeling uneasy about the invitation, she trudged into her apartment and sank onto the couch.

The ringing of the phone woke her up an hour later. It was Rick, just as he had promised. Immediately she again recognized the fear in his voice. "What do you want to do about this?" he instantly asked.

"I don't know," she mumbled. "The whole thing hasn't had time to sink in yet. What do you think?" She hoped he would be helpful in sorting out their options, for he had a knack for being able to stand back, remove himself from a situation, and rationally work through a problem.

"I've spent the past few hours thinking about nothing else," he said slowly. "You know that I care about you very much, and I will stick by you through whatever you decide to do. However, I don't think that marriage is an option to consider since neither one of us is up to raising a child." He paused. "We each already have a grown child, and we aren't as young as we used to be."

"Yes, you're a very old man," Karen snapped back, frustration in her voice. Realizing that they were getting off the subject, she forced herself to calm down. "Honestly, what are your thoughts?"

"Well, I have to be honest and say that my first choice would be abortion. We each have families and careers to be concerned about."

Abortion! Shock and anger engulfed her as the word echoed within her mind. It was bad enough that he had just admitted that he wouldn't even consider marriage—to take some sort of responsibility for the result of what they had done—but now, to add insult to injury, he spoke so casually about killing their child. Granted, an abortion had been one thought that had initially entered her mind as well, but coming from Rick it struck a nerve.

"I know that I don't hold the same beliefs on abortion as most Christians do." He seemed unsure what to say next.

"What do you believe?"

"I believe that a life begins when a child is old enough to survive on its own outside its mother."

What she was hearing stunned her. "Are you serious?" she asked in amazement. *Who is this man that I am speaking with?* Bewildered, she blinked. *This isn't the man that I love and hoped to marry one day. This has to be a bad dream. A very bad dream.*

"It's not really a baby yet, just a bunch of cells that will become a baby in weeks or months," Rick rambled on. Usually he was so logical, so rational, and she admired him for those qualities, yet now he just didn't make sense. Years ago babies would have died when born at 30 weeks. Now they lived when born at less than 20.

"Not a baby yet?" she exploded. "Where do you get that insane idea from? A baby is formed at conception. Haven't you seen a picture of a 10-week-old fetus?" Her heart raced ferociously as she forged ahead. "It has a brain, eyes, ears, and everything else. It's just tiny."

Part of a text flashed through her mind: "Before I formed you in the womb I knew you." Yes, there was no doubt in her mind that her baby was real, that it was living, and that God already had plans for the child's life.

"Calm down," he pleaded. "I'm only telling you what I believe so you'll know where I stand." Somehow Karen made herself listen, her body and mind numb. "I'm not trying to force you into anything."

"That's good." She struggled to form words. "Do you have any other ideas? I don't think I can go through with the first one."

"How would you feel about adoption?"

She began to cry softly. "I can't imagine doing that."

"The child deserves to be brought up in a loving home with parents who want it," he continued. "Our situation isn't ideal, any way you look at it. We're too old to be raising a child. Perhaps someone else could offer it more than we could."

Karen sighed heavily. "But that still doesn't solve the problem of our careers, and people finding out . . ." Her voice trailed off as hopelessness engulfed her.

"Well I don't know what to do, Karen," he said, trying to sound reassuring but coming across as irritated. "If you won't consider abortion, then I don't think there is an easy answer."

She was too upset to respond. After several moments each sensed that the other was at their breaking point. "It's late, and we're both exhausted," he said finally. "Let's get some sleep and talk more about this tomorrow."

After they said goodbye, Karen lay on the couch and longed for the peace that she had experienced earlier in the day. The terror in Rick's voice tonight had once again left her emotionally frazzled. Although she had hoped that he would be able to console her, as he usually could, all she felt now was frustration and confusion.

She needed someone to talk to. *Should I confide in Emily?* It was so tempting. But she knew the answer to her own question. If she did say anything to her, Grant would know too, and although he would be sympathetic, he might feel obligated to tell her employer.

Karen realized that she couldn't share her news with anyone. Not anyone. Yet just as she concluded that it was something that she and Rick must keep to themselves, she then remembered Sandy, a mutual friend of hers and Rick's that she'd met a few weeks earlier.

One of the first trips that she and Rick had taken together had been down to visit the woman that scheduled many of his concerts for him. Rick had known her for a couple of years, and she had been a big help to him with his music ministry.

Karen had spoken with her on the telephone several times before they had actually met. Commenting that the two women had a lot in common, especially in the area of divorce, Rick had suggested that they get to know each other. Occasionally he would make phone calls to Sandy while visiting Karen, and soon began putting Karen on the phone with her when he finished talking. The two enjoyed chatting, and Sandy often inquired how Karen was doing with her job and with her divorce, always offering words of encouragement.

Karen's mind wandered back to the first time that the two had actually seen each other. She and Rick had arrived at Sandy's house around 8:00 that Friday evening. Greeting them at the door with a big smile, Sandy exclaimed in her southern drawl, "Hey, ya'll! Come on in and make yourselves at home." As she gave Karen a big hug she said, "So nice to finally meet you."

In her late 30s, Sandy was divorced too. Standing a little over five feet tall, she always dressed impeccably, despite being overweight. Dark hair came to her shoulders and was styled nicely. Her face reminded Karen of a china doll—gorgeous and without blemish.

Once inside Sandy bubbled, "Let me show you to your rooms so that you can put your things away." Leading them up the stairs and pointing through an open door, she announced, "Rick, you'll have the master bedroom and bath." As she switched on the light she continued, "And Karen, you'll stay in my daughter's room since she is out of town for the weekend."

"But what about you?" he protested.

"I have the twin bed made up in the guest room, so I'm all set. I want you both to be comfortable."

What a gracious host, Karen smiled to herself.

Sandy had a flair for decorating, and the furniture and accessories in her brand new townhouse were beautiful. Each room had a coordinated wallpaper border, complemented by elegant crown molding and baseboard. Plush carpeting covered every floor except for the kitchen, bathrooms, and entryway, and she had those areas done in expensive tile. Each bedroom sported a specific color theme with matching bedspreads and drapes.

In addition to being a splendid host, Sandy was also a fabulous cook. She always prepared delightful meals ahead for the entire weekend. Sandy and Rick playfully joked about who was the best cook, and they attempted to get Karen in on the rivalry. "You're both the best," she responded with a smile, refusing to take sides.

A cozy fire crackled in the brick fireplace in the living room, and the smell of wood smoke hung faintly in the air. That evening Karen sat on the floor in front of Rick, enjoying a neck rub while the three chatted and made plans for the weekend. Although he had two concerts to do, they still had plenty of time left to relax and unwind.

During the Saturday evening concert Sandy and Karen sat halfway back in the auditorium. Glancing around, they enjoyed watching people. Some in the audience had their eyes closed during the quieter songs, as if in prayer. Others moved their lips, repeating the words. Frequently many would clap along during the more upbeat songs. In between numbers Rick would tell short stories and humorous anecdotes, and the people responded with laughter. Although he had done more than 3,000 concerts during the course of his ministry, he had a talent for keeping each one fresh and personal.

The number of women who, after learning that he was a bachelor, tried hitting on Rick after each concert amazed Karen. When everyone finally left, she and Sandy stood in the lobby packing up tapes and CDs. "Are the women always this way toward him?" Karen inquired. Sandy had sold tapes and CDs at many of Rick's concerts, and Karen imagined that she had seen it all.

"Yes, this is pretty typical. It must do a job on the ego to deal with this kind of attention all the time."

Karen felt totally comfortable with Sandy and never doubted that her friendship with Rick was platonic since she had been through a nasty divorce and had a difficult time trusting men after the abuse she had endured. With no reason to feel threatened by Sandy's relationship with him, Karen soon found herself wanting to become close to her as well.

As she stood in Sandy's daughter's room packing for the trip home, she reminisced about the visit. *This has been the best weekend that I've had in a long time.* She smiled to herself as she acknowledged that both Rick and Sandy had showered her with attention. *I like being spoiled.*

Sandy gave them both a hug as they prepared to leave. Rick squeezed her back and thanked her for her hospitality and support of his ministry. After giving Karen a second hug Sandy handed her a women's devotional Bible. "Here, I want you to have this," she began. "And I want you to call me if you ever need to talk."

Now those words echoed in Karen's ear. *Should I call her? Did God put her in my life for such a time as this?* she mused as a sense of peace once again returned. *Yes, I'll call Sandy soon,* she decided. Making that decision somehow strengthened her. Although it was a small decision, it was something—something that had been settled. Every little thing counted now, in a life that seemed to be rapidly spinning out of control.

With a sigh Karen now walked toward the door. Grant and Emily would be expecting her. Hoping that the knowledge that she could call Sandy would be enough to get her through the next hour without spilling her secret, she put on her shoes and turned off the lights.

The couple's front door was open when Karen arrived, so she just walked in. Closing the door behind her, she surveyed the room. The house was in its usual state of chaos. Toys, books, and stuffed animals were strewn across the living room floor. A half-eaten apple lay on the couch, wedged between the cushions. As she headed into the kitchen, Brent and Kaylee, who were running from their older brother, Brad, nearly ran over her. Laughing for the first time all day, Karen joined Emily at the stove. "How's it going?" she asked nonchalantly, hoping that the younger woman wouldn't return the question.

Emily rolled her eyes and laughed. "Same as always. Crazy." She wiped her hands. "How are you?" Before Karen could respond, the sound of breaking glass and a wail interrupted them. "Mommy!" Kaylee's shrill cry saved Karen from having to answer.

Rushing into the living room, Karen saw a vase shattered on the floor. "She did it," Brad pointed at Kaylee. "She hid under the table and it fell off!" His sister kept screaming.

Seeing the mess, Brent started picking up pieces of glass. Out of the corner of her eye, Karen saw him raise a fragment to his mouth. "Oh, no!" she exclaimed, rushing to the child and taking the shard out of his hand.

Kaylee was still crying. "It's not my fault!" Brad kept insisting.

"Just step back." Emily sounded exasperated. "I don't want you to get cut!" But the boys ignored her.

Karen kept her attention on Brent, who was still eyeing the glass shards with interest. "Come here, guys," she called. "Let's get some cookies from the kitchen." At the mention of food the boys forgot the glass and followed after her.

"Thanks," Emily called after her. Once she got the boys settled at the table with three chocolate chip cookies apiece, Karen went back into the living room where Emily was checking Kaylee for cuts. "Can you get the vacuum out of the closet?" she asked apologetically.

"No problem." She got it, and after helping Emily pick up the large pieces, vacuumed the floor for anything they had missed. *I bet this is the first vacuuming this floor has had in months,* Karen thought absentmindedly as the machine sucked up hair, dirt, and shreds of paper.

"Thank you," Emily sighed, standing.

"Mommy!" Brad screamed. Emily rushed into the kitchen. Water was bubbling from the pot on the stove and running down onto the floor.

"Oh, no!" Emily shrieked. She hurtled toward the stove and turned the burner off. Brad started toward her. "Stay away! It'll burn you!"

Just then the phone rang. Emily looked pleadingly at Karen. "I'll get it," Karen said. "Grant," she called a moment later, "Steve Gardner is on the phone!"

Emily's husband hurried down the stairs. "Thanks," he said, grabbing the phone.

"I'm hungry!" Brent announced.

"Me too!" Brad and Kaylee chimed in.

"Honey, where is our insurance file?" Grant asked, holding one hand over the receiver.

"I don't know!" Emily replied, her frustration evident in her voice.

"You organized the office," he reminded her.

"Mommy!" Kaylee tugged at her leg. "I'm hungry!"

"Wait a minute," Emily snapped at her. The child burst into tears. From the next room came a baby's cry. Katie had awakened.

Witnessing the scene, Karen thought back to when Sarah had been a toddler and had the habit of taking off her diaper and walking around the house waving it like a flag. She remembered those hectic evenings when the phone kept ringing, and she was trying to make supper, keep Sarah clothed, and hold on to her sanity. And that was only one child! Suddenly remembering her dilemma, which she had temporarily forgotten in the pandemonium, Karen panicked at the thought of handling the demands of motherhood again. *Can I do it?* she asked herself, suddenly feeling tired. *Do I want to? Is it worth it?* She glanced at Emily, who looked as if she were about to cry. "I think I'll go home . . ." Karen motioned toward the door.

Emily nodded. "Sorry about this," the woman sighed. "Come back later if you want, when the kids are in bed." Karen headed for the door, glad that at least for now, her apartment was peaceful and quiet.

WEEK 11

Karen could not take her eyes off the girl. About a year old, she was sitting on a blanket in the park, wearing a green spring dress and white sandals. Her dark hair shone, highlighting a hint of natural curl. Magnificent brown eyes sparkled, dancing with excitement as she played with the golden retriever puppy. Her lop-sided smile showcased several baby teeth. The puppy, licking her face playfully, frolicked around, and the child giggled as she rolled on the blanket. Karen, standing in the shadows of a large willow tree, felt herself drawn to the girl. *Where is her mother? Maybe she is . . .*

The alarm clock jolted Karen wake. Rubbing her eyes, she sat up and tried to gain her bearings, the images of the beautiful child, the sunshine, and the puppy still etched in her mind.

As she drifted in and out of sleep all night, fears had consumed Karen even in her dreams. Several times she had awakened to discover tears on her cheeks and her pillowcase wet.

This can't be real! It just can't be real! She pounded her pillow with her fists. Her body ached from sobbing, and her mind felt heavy and numb. Realizing that she'd never be able to function at work, Karen reset the alarm for 8:00 a.m. so that she could call in sick. Turning onto her stomach she closed her bloodshot eyes and pulled the sheets up around her neck. *What am I going to do? How will I be able to do my work—or even live my life?* The questions beat through her mind. Suddenly, she remembered Sandy's invitation to call. She desperately needed to talk with someone and felt she could trust her. However, Karen didn't want to bother her unnecessarily and decided to verify the pregnancy first. *I'm going to call my doctor first thing this morning.*

The nurse summoned her from the door of the waiting room. Following the woman down the long hallway, Karen concentrated on putting one foot in front of the other. Fleetingly she wondered if prisoners on their way to execution felt anymore afraid.

Her heart raced, slowed, fluttered like a wounded bird against her throat. *This is it,* she thought. *Whatever the doctor says will be truth.* She had a wild urge to turn and flee to her car. Instead she kept her eyes on the vinyl tile floor and the shoes that followed the nurse, one foot, then the other.

Small and sterile, the room held a gray examining table, a steel chair with a pink vinyl cushion, and a sink with limited counter space. Gray tile covered the floor, and one fluorescent light was mounted on the ceiling. A few posters hung on the white walls. Karen stared at the one showing a baby's development throughout the nine months of pregnancy. Suddenly she felt herself back 18 years in time, joyfully pregnant with Sarah. She'd studied those charts with great excitement back then, eager to track her baby's growth and progress.

"What are you here for today?" the young, dark-haired, heavy-set nurse asked cheerfully, opening Karen's chart.

"I'd like a pregnancy test," she said hesitantly. "I've taken two at home, but I think there's some kind of mistake."

Guessing what the situation might be, the nurse calmly replied, "The doctor will be in shortly, and he can decide what tests should be ordered." Handing her a blue-and-white cotton gown, she continued, "Undress from the waist down. He'll be in soon."

As Karen undressed, fear was bitter in her throat. Her mouth was dry, her palms damp and cold. As she climbed onto the examining table the paper crinkled noisily when she sat down nervously on the edge. She bit her nails as she waited.

Dr. Jacobson knocked and then hurried into the room. He was in his mid-40s with brown wavy hair and sparkling blue eyes. His gentle demeanor had impressed Karen the first time that she had met him, almost a year earlier. Smiling, he asked, "What can I do for you today?"

"I'd like a pregnancy test. I took two at home, but I don't think they're right."

The doctor looked at her a moment. "Karen, these tests aren't wrong, at least if they're positive. Occasionally I've seen false negatives, but never a false positive." He opened her chart and then continued, "The nurse noted that you don't know when your last period was."

Shaking her head, Karen said, "No."

"OK. Well let's examine you and see what's going on." He pushed a button on the wall, and soon the nurse returned to the room. The doctor tried to make small talk during the exam, but Karen remained quiet. A few minutes later he took off his gloves and propped himself up against the sink as the nurse quietly left the room. Karen sat up and searched his eyes for an answer. Her heart raced as she folded and re-folded her damp hands.

"I know you don't want to hear this," he began cautiously, "but you're 11-weeks pregnant."

Her heart sank as tears streamed down her cheeks. This had been her last hope, the last chance to believe that it might be just a bad dream.

Dr. Jacobson walked over and took her hand. "Why are you so upset about this?" he questioned. "Although you're older than most women who have babies, you aren't 40 yet and should have a healthy pregnancy."

"The father doesn't want a baby—he's already told me that," she hiccupped, wiping her eyes. "And I'm not sure that I do either." After a short pause she added, "I'll be 40 in a couple years, my daughter is 17 and for the most part on her own, and I enjoy my career and freedom. I know that sounds selfish, but it's true."

"Then are you considering abortion?"

"Right now I'm exploring all options. Although I'm pretty sure I couldn't bring myself to have one." Her head was swimming. "Tell me about the procedure—what they do and what the risks are."

The doctor pulled up a chair. "Usually an abortion is performed by a technique called vacuum aspiration." His voice was neutral. "Under local anesthesia, a doctor dilates the cervix with an instrument so that it opens up enough for a small hollow tube to be inserted, and then with suction he will remove the contents of the uterus."

Stunned, she sat with her mind awhirl. *It all sounds so sterile and unreal. The contents of the uterus were really a baby!*

"If you make that choice, you must do it immediately." His tone still remained nonjudgmental. "The earlier the better, but since you are already 11 weeks along you don't have much time. Twelve weeks is the standard cut-off point."

The news left her short of breath. She had to make a choice soon. Overwhelmed with panic, she headed home. Listening to a southern gospel CD, she longed to lose herself in the music. On the drive home she passed a road sign that read "Pritchard Lane." It reminded her of Rick's favorite cousin, Patty, whose last name was Pritchard. Patty and her husband were a loving and energetic couple who had never been able to have children. *Perhaps they should raise this baby.* Shocked, she couldn't believe her thoughts. *Where did that come from?* she wondered. *Would they . . . ?*

Home again, Karen sat down in the wooden chair in front of her computer to check her e-mail. Two messages. One was from Sandy—a quick note of encouragement regarding Karen's divorce. A few words from her always brightened Karen's day. The other was from Sarah. Startled, Karen was suddenly hesitant to open it, as a host of thoughts flooded through her mind. Realizing the cause of her panic, she told herself, *Calm down! She doesn't know anything.* Then she couldn't help but laugh at her foolishness. Clicking on the button she read the long, detailed message. Sarah wrote about how her classes were progressing, offered some chit-chat about her friends and what they were up to, and toward the end inquired how her mother was doing.

As she shut down the computer, Karen felt a wave of relief in knowing that her daughter wouldn't be coming home anytime soon. She needed time to solve this problem—time to figure out what she wanted to do. Dropping onto her couch, she lay there and began reviewing her options. *Stay organized,* she reminded herself.

Abortion? It would be the easiest solution, an instant remedy that would allow me to get back my former life. Remembering her earlier conversation with the doctor, as well as testimonials that she had previously read about women who had become emotionally scarred after an abortion, Karen winced as the vivid details flashed through her mind. While she wished that she could forget those facts and go ahead with the procedure, deep down she realized that she couldn't. *I'd carry that guilt forever. And what would Sarah think if she ever found out?*

Adoption? Karen pondered the idea. *I don't think I could do it. How could I grow and nurture a baby through nine months of pregnancy, feel her move and kick, and then give her to someone else once she's born?* As she remembered the dream, the thought of the resulting heartache was more than she could handle, and a deep pain throbbed in her chest.

Plus, I'll have to find another job, since I'll get fired from my current position. Karen enjoyed working with teenagers, and it was particularly nice to help them within a Christian setting that allowed her to speak openly about her faith. Working in the public sector would mean significant change in her counseling approach.

And how will I ever tell my family? I know this will disappoint them. The faces of her brother and sister, as well as Sarah, flashed through her mind. Each would be shocked and hurt. Karen's parents had died in an automobile accident when she was 22, so she didn't have that additional pressure. *Once the nine months are up I could get back to somewhat of a normal life.* That part appealed to her.

Keeping the baby? Her thoughts pressed on. *If I keep her, I know I'll have to raise her myself.* Eighteen years flashed before her eyes, overwhelming her. *Plus, I'll still have to find another job . . . And I'll still have to face Sarah.* Her head ached as she realized that there was no easy answer.

The phone grabbed her attention. "Hello."

"Hi, how are you holding up?" Rick inquired. "I called your work, and they told me you were sick today."

"There's no way I could go to work. I didn't sleep much last night." She hesitated. "I went to see my doctor today."

"And?"

"I'm 11-weeks pregnant." Tears flowed as she heard herself say the words aloud. Somehow speaking about it made it seem so much more real.

"So this is for real, no doubt about it," he said as if the truth had suddenly hit him as well. "I've been praying for most of the night, making a lot of promises to God if He would just allow this to be a mistake."

"Me too." She and Rick were so much alike.

"Listen, I'm going to get in my car right now and drive out there. I'll be there by dinnertime, and we can continue sorting this out together. OK? I don't have any concerts until next weekend, and I can postpone the paperwork and other projects that I'm working on until another time."

"You don't have to come," she began, although she was relieved to know that he would be on his way soon. "What time did you get back from Virginia?"

"I flew in about midnight. Anyway, we've got a lot to work out, and it'll be easier if I'm there. See you in a few hours."

Karen longed for a firm hug from him. *Somehow he'll make things better,* she reassured herself. She remembered a time when one of his friends was going through a divorce, her husband physically abusing her. Rick had taken charge, rented a moving truck, and moved her and her children from the house while the husband was at work. He'd continued to provide moral support through many follow-up phone calls. Always the solid rock for friends and family, he constantly helped and encouraged others. Once she'd asked him about it, and with a smile he'd said, "It's an important part of my ministry." Now she hoped he would be the support she needed.

Looking for something to occupy her time until he arrived, Karen walked over to Emily's house. Something was always happening there: children playing, clothes to be folded, people coming and going, and Emily's never-ending cooking endeavors. She was a good cook and made everything from scratch, so the house was always filled with an inviting aroma, especially now that she had only one child in diapers.

"It's me," Karen announced after knocking and then walking through the front door.

"Come on in. I'm in the kitchen," Emily called from the adjacent room. "Why aren't you at work?" she asked as Karen entered the room.

"I wasn't feeling very good today, and so I called in sick. I think it's just the stress from the divorce."

"Well, have a seat and talk to me." Emily had pots and pans strewn all over the countertop as she worked on preparing supper. A crib now sat in the corner of the kitchen, Katie asleep in it. At six months she already bore a strong resemblance to her mother. Tears welled in Karen's eyes as suddenly the sight of a child had a whole new meaning.

Attempting not to break down, she quickly asked, "Could I borrow one of your videos? I think it's one of those days when I just need to be alone and watch something funny."

"Sure. You know where they are. Help yourself."

Grateful for Emily's preoccupation with cooking and children, Karen quickly chose one and excused herself before attracting unwanted questions. As she left, she thought that her friend had looked at her strangely. Did she suspect? *She can't know,* Karen reassured herself. *It's impossible.* Back in her apartment she popped in the video.

Rick arrived a few hours later and knocked on the door before entering. "Anybody home?" his deep voice echoed. A bit nervous, Karen's heart raced as she got up off the couch.

Instead of the big hug she had been expecting, Rick cautiously put his arms around her and barely squeezed, letting go quickly.

Stunned, she didn't know how to react. Two days worth of stress and anxiety had taken their toll on her emotions, not to mention the pregnancy hormones surging throughout her body. Her eyes, brimming with tears, darted around the room as she let him have it. "I'm not dying, you know! I won't break if you hug me!" She looked up at him and abruptly stopped ranting, staring in disbelief at the tears in his eyes.

Grabbing her firmly, he hugged her tightly as his body shook with emotion. For a long time they cried and held each other, not knowing what else to do. "I can't believe this is happening!" she sobbed.

Rick squeezed her harder. "It'll be OK," he reassured her, but his fear was evident. His voice shook.

Finally, after regaining his composure, he hugged her one more time, then led her to the couch. "Here, rest a while, and I'll make supper. Does spaghetti sound OK to you?"

"Sounds good. I haven't eaten all day."

Conversation over dinner was sparse, and halfway through they moved to the living room so that they could watch television. Both were relieved to have something to focus on besides each other and the discussion they could not avoid forever.

After the meal, she volunteered to do the dishes while he relaxed on the couch. As she cleared the table, she glanced into the living room. His dark hair and broad shoulders were all she could see as he stretched out on the couch, flipping through the channels with the remote control. Since he usually chose one program and watched it intently, she surmised that he wasn't paying attention to anything on the screen as he continued to spend only a minute or two on each channel before clicking to the next.

Karen washed every dish. Then she dried every dish. Slowly she wiped down each countertop. Finally she gathered the garbage and took the bag down the hall to the trash room. How she dreaded walking into the living room and facing reality. Looking around the kitchen for anything that she had missed, she folded the hand towel and the dishcloth, procrastinating a few more moments.

Finally she could stall no more. Rick turned off the television and sat up as she walked in and sat awkwardly on the edge of the couch.

Glancing nervously at her, he took the initiative. "There appear to be three solutions to this problem," he began in his *I'm going to solve all of the world's problems* tone of voice. His take-charge approach comforted her. *Good,* she thought, *he's going to come up with a solution.* She listened intently as he continued. "Our options are abortion, adoption, or keeping the child." Karen noticed how he always referred to the baby as "the child" and wondered if it was a hint of denial. *How cold he can be at times,* she noted.

Before she had a chance to comment he added, "I still think that abortion is our best solution, considering our ages and the nature of our work." Pausing for a minute, he held her hand. "Unless you have an abortion, this will definitely destroy both of our careers, there's no way around it." He looked pleadingly at her.

"I know, I know!" she exploded, jerking her hand from his. "That's all that's been on my mind since I found out I'm pregnant! There's so much pressure in my head right now, I can't even think."

"Calm down," Rick begged. "Let's keep talking and work through this."

Taking a deep breath and slowly regaining her composure, she resumed in a softer tone, "On the way home from the doctor's office I had a thought. How would you feel about giving the baby to Patty and her husband, since they've never been able to have children?"

"Absolutely not!" His face reddened as he stood up and began pacing. "I don't want our families to know about this."

"Why not?" she asked, perplexed by his adamant no. "Can't we even talk about this? If I don't have an abortion, they're going to find out anyway! Why not consider giving the baby to Patty?"

Ignoring her he continued to pace. Not saying anything, she watched him. She knew that this could go on for days, since they were both extremely strong-willed.

Finally Rick broke the silence. "We're both tired, and maybe we should continue working on this tomorrow. Let's pray together and then watch TV or something and unwind."

They held hands as they knelt in the stillness of the living room. "Dear Father," Rick began. "Thank You for Your blessings. Thank You for being there for us during the bad times as well as the good. As You know, we have a big problem, and we don't know what to do." He paused and squeezed her hand gently. "You know that we have already prayed for forgiveness for our sin, and we believe that You have already done that. But Lord, I ask You to work this problem out now." Nervously he continued, "Please, dear Father, allow Karen to miscarry." Without thinking she smiled to herself. She had already prayed that same prayer. "And if not, at least show us what to do. Amen."

Although they had prayed together many times throughout their relationship, this time felt so different. They were like children in trouble, begging a parent to fix things and make it all better again.

"Rick," she began softly as they sat back down on the couch. "During prayer I was reminded that what we are going through is a result—a natural consequence—of our sin. I've been blaming God for something that we got ourselves into, and I imagine that you have too." The weight of that realization made it difficult for her to breathe.

"I know," he conceded nervously. "But I'm so tired. Please let's just do something else and save the talking for tomorrow."

As they watched television, Rick lay on the couch and Karen sat in the green chair, feet propped up over one of its arms. Eventually she realized that he was no longer commenting on the program and glanced over at him, noting that he had fallen asleep.

After turning off the television, she stared at him for a few minutes, observing the outline of his features. Even in his sleep he appeared restless, a tense look on his face, as his body twitched every few minutes. Vacillating between hope and despair, she wondered what the outcome of their situation would be. Although they hadn't found an acceptable solution yet, she held onto a strand of hope since they cared deeply for each other and were committed to protecting their careers. With this common ground she hoped that they'd figure out something soon. *Please God,* she began to pray—the same prayer she'd been repeating for the past couple days.

After covering Rick with a blanket, she turned off the light, and went to bed. However, sleep was elusive, and she tossed and turned. *Maybe an abortion is the best option,* she tried to convince herself. No one would ever have to know. *Take a day or two off from work, get it done, and go back to life as usual.* It was a tempting solution. *Surely God would rather us have an abortion than cause a scandal and ruin the work we're doing for Him,* she reasoned. With that thought in mind, she finally fell asleep.

As she prepared for work the next morning, she tiptoed around so as not to awaken Rick. Exhausted, she wondered where she'd find the energy to do her job. Shocked at how pale she looked, she dabbed on more makeup.

Just as she was opening the door to leave, she heard Rick ask groggily from the couch, "What time will you be back?"

Karen looked at her watch after retracing her steps to the living room. "I'm going to try to leave early, around 3:00 or so. I've gotta get going now though, or I'll be late."

The day dragged by, and it took all her energy to put on a smile and to pretend that everything was fine. Thankful for an office in a back part of the building, she stayed there most of the time, working on a mindless project due the following week and avoiding contact with coworkers or students. *Just do what I have to do,* she told herself. *One day at a time.*

Later, as she gathered her things to leave the office, Jenni, a dark-haired and vivacious senior, sauntered into the office. "Hey, Karen," the girl chirped. "Just wanted to say hi!"

"Hi, Jenni," Karen forced herself to say. "How are you?"

"Good," she responded cheerfully. "Josh and I have been dating for one year today!" Karen couldn't help but smile. They weren't the typical 17-year-olds hanging all over each other or breaking up and getting back together every three weeks.

"Doing anything for your anniversary?" Karen asked, determined to focus on something besides her own problem. *Act cheerful,* she reminded herself.

"He's coming to my house this weekend."

"Sounds like fun."

"Yeah, I'm excited. Gotta run to get to class. See you tomorrow." Jenni hurried out the door and down the hall. Stopping by the office several times a week, the girl would talk about her boyfriend, her classes, and her friends. Karen had always enjoyed the conversations. It reminded her of when she had been young and everything seemed so important. She remembered the devastation of her first breakup—at 15—and how she had been positive the world was ending. If she had only known then that someday she would be strong enough to survive the end of a marriage. And now this! The thought of when her best friend had become pregnant two months before graduation suddenly popped into her mind. The girl had kept anyone from finding out until she had her diploma. Then she had married the father. That marriage lasted four years. Sadly Karen shook her head. *This is no way to start out a marriage.* Marrying Rick was not an option—not under present circumstances.

Making an excuse to leave early, she arrived home a little after 3:00. As she cautiously opened the door to her apartment, she could hear one of her favorite CDs playing on the stereo, and Rick harmonizing along with the song. Tiptoeing to the entrance of the living room and propping herself against the door case, she watched him as he stood in front of the big picture window, staring outside, singing to himself.

His voice soothed her. Effortlessly he harmonized high and low, emotion flooding from his soul. The message of grace in the song filled her with hope and encouragement.

When the song ended he turned around, startled to find her standing there. "How was your day?" he asked, walking over to the couch and sitting down.

"I survived. Basically I avoided everyone." Taking a seat beside him, she looked into his face. The tired and frightened look in his eyes surprised her, and she didn't know how to respond. "What about you?"

"I did a lot of thinking," he began, playing with a pen, avoiding her eyes.

"Any new ideas?" she asked hopefully. Surely he had come up with something.

"I'm more and more convinced that abortion is our only option. It's the only way to keep this a secret and not destroy our careers." He glanced at her, waiting for her reaction. His voice was hard, cold.

"Rick, that's the one thing I can't do. Yes, it would solve our immediate problems but create others in the long run. I don't think I can live with that choice."

"Please!" His voice broke. "Do this for me." He worked to remain calm, breathing deeply and constantly shifting position. "My ministry is my entire life. If word of this gets out, my career is ruined, and then what will I do? At my age, jobs aren't plentiful." The panic in his voice shook her. *He's even more scared than I am,* she realized with surprise. *But how can he be so demanding, so insensitive? Sure, I thought about abortion last night, but I know I can't do it. I know it can't be what God wants. Can't he realize that it's just trying to fix one sin with another?*

"Don't pressure me!" she begged in frustration. "Let me change my clothes, then I'll be back."

As resentment welled up in her she could barely breathe. Taking her time changing, Karen dreaded returning to the living room. As she sat on the edge of the bed, she looked up at the ceiling. *God, when are the answers going to come?* she pleaded. *Where is the man that I used to know and love? Why is Rick so different now—so uncaring and selfish?* Her heart ached as she wiped away a tear. *Everything is falling apart.*

A few minutes later she strode into the living room in her jeans and a large burgundy sweat shirt. *Try to stay calm,* she told herself.

"Feeling better?"

"I always feel better in my jeans." Sitting on the couch, she pulled her feet up under her and placed her arm on the back of the couch, glancing sideways at him.

"Are you thinking about keeping the child?" he asked, his eyes focused on the floor in front of him. "I need to know what you're planning."

Silence. Karen wasn't sure where to begin. "I've run through the three scenarios in my mind again and again. I keep wishing that something new would jump out at me." Her chin quivered as she struggled to maintain her composure, but she spoke slowly and deliberately. "Deep down I know I can't go through with an abortion, yet the other two ideas don't seem feasible either."

Rick leaned forward on the couch, his head in his hands. In a muffled tone he asked, "If I'm convinced that abortion is the only solution, and you refuse to have one, then what's the point in talking anymore?"

Without saying a word, she slid closer and put her hand on his neck. He jumped when she touched him. Beginning to massage his neck and shoulders, she slowly felt the muscles loosen a little. Sitting in the quietness of the living room, each lost in their individual thoughts, she kneaded until her hands were tired.

Rick broke the silence, "How long do you think you can hide the pregnancy before someone finds out?"

"I don't know. Why?" she asked, puzzled.

"I just want to know how long I have before my world, as I currently know it, goes down the drain," he answered in despair.

Are you really that selfish? Karen numbly wondered to herself. *Don't you have any feelings for anyone but yourself?* Tears brimmed, yet she refused to let them flow. "Listen, we're two intelligent adults. There must be a solution that we're missing."

"Yeah? Like what?"

"I don't know. Maybe I could get a job overseas. Or take an extended leave-of-absence." She paused for a moment and with a gleam in her eye continued, "What if I were to tell people that I'm a surrogate mother?"

Slowly he turned toward her, an intrigued expression glistening in his eyes. "Do you think that might work?" Hope had returned to his voice.

"Honestly? I doubt it. Without talking about those kinds of plans with my coworkers and family well in advance, it would be so unexpected that they probably wouldn't buy it. But it's worth considering." She giggled at the thought, surprised to hear herself laughing.

"My brain is so tired right now," Rick said in an exasperated tone. "Let's order pizza and not talk about this anymore tonight."

Karen nodded. "Mine hurts too."

After eating Rick seemed to become on edge and preoccupied once again. "Karen, for the past two days we've worked at solving this problem. But it seems as if we're at a stalemate. I think it might help if I went home so that we each had some time to think and pray by ourselves."

Shocked, she stared at him. "I guess I thought that we'd come up with something before you left." Tears welled up again, and with a sinking feeling in her stomach she sadly concluded, "Perhaps there isn't a solution." Turning around to face the back of the couch, she buried her head in her arms as she wept in despair. *Dear God, where are You now? Is he really going to leave me like this?*

A text flashed through her mind. *"I will never leave you or forsake you." Well, at least I know that You won't leave me, Father. Hold me tight. Please comfort me right now.*

Rick began to rub her back. "We'll work this out together, I promise," he began. "But I . . . we each need space right now—to think and pray individually." He continued to massage her back as her body calmed and normal, rhythmic breathing returned. "I'll call every night."

WEEK 12

Worn out after a long day at work, Karen slumped onto the couch and reached for the cordless phone on the stand beside the couch, but it rang before she touched it. Startled, she paused, hand in mid-air, wondering if it was Rick, calling each day as he'd promised. With a deliberate effort to shake off her exhaustion, she picked up the receiver. "Hello." She shifted to get more comfortable, pulling her legs up against her.

"Hi, Karen." Sandy's soft southern accent was distinctive. "I haven't heard from you in a while and was wondering how you're doing."

"I was just reaching for the phone to call *you!*" Karen tried to be upbeat.

"What's new? I haven't heard from you or Rick in more than a week," Sandy chuckled, "and that's unusual."

"It's been a busy week for us," Karen said cautiously. *If only she knew! How can I break this to her?*

"Oh?"

"You've been on my mind a lot. I've been going through so much and have been meaning to call." Her voice broke on the last words.

"What's going on?"

Tears flowed. "It's been the worst week of my life!"

"Karen, you sound terrible. What's happened?" Sandy demanded.

Swallowing, her throat dry, she attempted to force the words out. For a second she hesitated, breathing deeply, then plunged ahead. Might as well just spit it out. "I'm pregnant." Sobs shook her body as salty tears streamed down her cheeks. *All I do is cry,* she thought to herself. *I cry all the time!*

"What?" Sandy exclaimed. After a lengthy silence, she said, "Oh Karen, I'm so sorry."

"Me too," Karen said flatly, reaching for a tissue. "I can't believe this is happening!"

"Oh my!" Sandy moaned audibly. "What are you guys planning to do?"

"Good question." Now that all was out in the open, Karen felt more in control of herself. "We've been trying to figure that out all week. Rick came down for a couple days to talk, but there doesn't seem to be a solution that we can agree upon."

"You could come down here and have a small ceremony. I could help put things together for a wedding."

"No. We've discussed many options, and marriage isn't one of them," Karen sighed. "Marriages that begin because of pregnancy rarely work, and neither one of us have a good track record with marriage in the first place."

"Then what are you considering?" Sandy asked cautiously.

"Rick wants me to have an abortion." Karen caught her breath, wondering what her friend's reaction would be. "We've also discussed adoption, as well as raising the baby."

Sandy ignored Karen's reference to abortion. "With Rick's ministry, that must make this choice even harder."

"Yes, it does. It seems that a solution doesn't exist that won't destroy either our lives or our careers—or both. Rick and I are trying to be strong for each other, but it's tough when we're both scared and frustrated. I just don't know . . ." Her voice trailed off.

"What can I do to help?" Her tone remained nonjudgmental.

"How about going to Maine with me this coming weekend? I have the use of a friend's cabin on the ocean, and I could use some time away—and a friend to talk to."

Sandy said nothing for a few seconds. "I can't think of anything I have to do during the weekend. Sure, I can get away."

"Good! I'll e-mail you directions." A wave of relief washed over Karen. Here at last was a chance to escape from her apartment and spend time talking to someone more objective.

• • • •

Excited about the possibility of a weekend away, Karen left for Maine early that Friday. She loved the ocean. It had brought her solace in the past, and she hoped that it would again. *I need something,* she cried out inside. *I need help . . .*

Arriving at the beachfront cottage around 2:00, she almost missed the small dirt driveway hidden by large pine trees. As she drove her dark blue Volvo down the quarter-mile-long drive, the car bounced from the many potholes on the narrow, winding road.

Parking beside the cottage, Karen caught a whiff of the salty ocean air. She breathed deeply, then inhaled again, smiling. *Oh, this is heaven!* The sunshine glistened off the waves rhythmically beating against the rocky shoreline. She could hear each wave's thunderous roar. The screams of seagulls punctuated the sound of the surf.

Carrying her brown leather overnight bag and a sack of groceries toward the house, Karen studied the cabin. She'd been there several times before, but it always intrigued her. It was a small, one-story shingled structure with plenty of windows. Age and the elements had bleached the overlapping cedar shingles into numerous shades of gray. The loose green shutter flapping in the breeze was surprising on what was otherwise a well-maintained structure. A wide stone chimney towered above the center of the roof.

She was grateful for the high school friend that had let her use the cabin occasionally. Suzanne, always focused and ambitious throughout high school, had gone on to become a successful stockbroker in New York City. They'd kept in touch through occasional e-mails and Christmas cards.

Setting her bags down, Karen reached for the key hidden under a cement planter to the left of the door. One turn and the door swung open. A stale smell engulfed her as she entered, an indication that Suzanne didn't spend much time there. She left the front door propped open a little and then unlatched the back door, cracking it a bit, letting fresh air circulate.

Almost the entire back of the cabin was large windows and a huge deck ran along the entire structure. A good-sized living room with a stone fireplace sat directly in the center. The small functional kitchen was immediately to the left. A bathroom was tucked in over to the right. Two bedrooms, nestled in the back corners of the cabin, sat across from each other, both with a stunning view of the water.

After putting her things away in the bedroom closest to the bathroom, Karen returned to the living room and gazed out at the ocean. Since Sandy wouldn't arrive for another hour or two, she decided to walk down by the water. It was chilly, and she grabbed her windbreaker before heading out the door.

A small overgrown trail led from the porch down to the ocean a few hundred feet away. The path, covered by uneven stone, odd bricks, and lined with wood planks, disappeared in spots. Grass had grown up through the rocks, and bushes, even though they had lost their leaves a few weeks earlier, sometimes obscured the path.

As Karen walked beside the water, she mulled over her situation and options. The fact that she was entering her twelfth week of pregnancy intensified her anxiety.

Sitting on a large boulder beside the water, she braced her elbows on her knees and rested her chin in her hands. Gazing skyward she prayed, *Father, please allow me to have rest and peace this weekend.* She watched the seagulls as they dove in and out from between the rocks. *And be with Rick, too. I know he has concerts, and this pressure is really getting to him.* Choking back the tears, she thought, *I don't want this to destroy him or his ministry, dear Father. Please! Don't let that happen!* she begged. *I promise, I'll . . .* But she couldn't think of anymore promises to make.

For almost an hour she sat there, breathing in the salt air and praying. Understanding that half of the purpose of prayer is listening for God to speak, she took turns verbalizing her thoughts and desires and questions, then remaining quiet, awaiting His response.

During one of those quiet moments her thoughts returned to when God had spoken to her during the last time that she and Rick had prayed together. *What we are going through is a result . . . a natural consequence . . . of our sin.* She knew that God did not enjoy punishing people—the Bible was clear about that. *Didn't Jeremiah say, "For I know the thoughts I think of you . . . thoughts of peace and not evil, to give you a future and a hope?" Yes, I know that You want the best for me, dear Lord. You have provided guidelines to spare me from situations just like this. This pain is a result of sin—my sin.* A feeling of warmth flooded her. *This is what being intimate with God is all about.*

Somehow, she believed that God was in control, even if she was not.

Finally, glancing at her watch she realized it was time to head back to the cabin. She wanted to put the frozen lasagna into the oven so that it would be ready for dinner that evening. Sandy taught fifth and sixth grade at a small elementary school. Although she had managed to find a substitute for her classroom that Friday, she had to stop by the school and go over the assignments with the other woman before leaving for Maine.

Inside, after she had the lasagna in the oven, she plunked down on the couch directly across from the large windows in the living room, propping her feet up cautiously on the coffee table. Made from a large, weather-beaten lobster trap, its wood had turned gray over time. A solid piece of glass lay across the top. Eventually a horn honked, interrupting her thoughts. Excitedly she hurried to the door. "Hey, you found it!" Karen exclaimed, hugging Sandy tightly.

After showing her to her room, Karen asked, "How many hours did it take you?"

"Seven."

Pausing for a few minutes to stare out the large windows at the ocean, Sandy exclaimed, "This is so beautiful! Let's sit on the deck a while before it gets too dark."

They relaxed in matching dark green wooden Adirondack lounge chairs until the sun set slowly behind them. Finally Sandy pulled her coat up around her neck. "Brrrrr, it's chilly out here, but so beautiful." Glancing at Karen, she asked, "How's Sarah?"

A smile spread across Karen's face. "She loves the student exchange program! They get to travel regularly, plus she's doing well with her studies. How's Aubrey?" She was Sandy's teenage daughter.

"Doing fine. I can't believe she's a freshman in high school, though."

"And Dan?"

"He's a senior this year—makes me feel old." Sandy chuckled, then became somber. "Will Sarah be home for Christmas?"

The question caught Karen off guard. "No. She'll be there all year." Suddenly she realized that something that had once made her feel sad was actually a relief now. She didn't want her daughter to see her now.

"What are you going to tell her about all this?" Sandy asked carefully.

Karen sat up straight in the lounge chair, leaned forward, and pulled her legs up close to her, putting her arms around them. As she gazed at the ocean, she said, "I don't know." Her voice cracked. Tears flowed down her cheeks as she buried her head in her arms and rocked back and forth.

Sandy got up from her chair and sat down beside Karen, her arm around her friend's shoulder. Sobbing, Karen could not speak. "It's OK," Sandy said. "I can't imagine what you're going through."

Eventually Karen pulled a tissue from her coat pocket and wiped her eyes and blew her nose. "Thanks for being here for me." Attempting a smile, she continued, "I'll try not to cry on you all weekend." The two hugged, then laughed as they made their way inside.

Dinner consisted of lasagna, salad, and brownies, served on purple and yellow paper plates with matching cups. Sandy chuckled as she threw out the disposable plates and slipped the leftover lasagna into the refrigerator. "Wow, this was an easy clean up!"

Karen grinned. "Yes, after your large dinner parties and being the perfect hostess, this meal must seem pretty simple."

As the women sat and relaxed in the small living room, the cries of seagulls and the booms of waves crashing echoed from outside. "Karen," Sandy smiled shyly, "what is it that first attracted you to Rick?"

Changing positions in the green chair, Karen smiled to herself. "I guess it was because he was everything that my ex-husband wasn't."

Sandy's eyes lit up. "Oh? What do you mean?"

"Well, music was the biggest thing. I've loved music all of my life—learned to play the piano when I was 7 and have written songs ever since." After sipping from her water bottle, she continued. "Plus, Rick has a strong work ethic, which I admire. He works from the time he wakes up until he drops at night." Her smile broadened as she added, "Also, he makes me believe that I can do anything. He has a confidence in me that my ex-husband never had."

"Yes, Rick has many good qualities. I was curious what brought you two together."

Before long Karen started to yawn repeatedly. "I'm so tired," she said, covering her mouth as another one began. "I'm going to bed even though it's early. I hope you understand."

"Absolutely! I'm going to read for a while, but I'm sure I won't last long either."

As sunshine streamed through her window the next morning Karen stretched and then snuggled deeper under the comforter, glad that she didn't have to get up until she wanted to. Hearing noises from the kitchen, she realized that Sandy must already be making breakfast. *I guess I should get up, as much as I'd like to stay tucked away all morning.* Pulling on her robe, she walked slowly to the kitchen.

"Good morning," Sandy greeted her. She'd already showered and dressed and appeared to be wide-awake.

Yawning, Karen opened the refrigerator. "How'd you sleep?"

"Fine. This ocean air is invigorating." Sandy smiled as she put some bread in the toaster. "Do you want something to eat—or do you get morning sickness?"

"I've been lucky so far and haven't been sick," Karen said after untwisting the cap of a bottle and taking a few sips. "I brought some breakfast patties that I'll fry up. Want some?"

"Sure."

After eating, Karen showered and dressed while Sandy sat on the deck and read a book. Although it was a late fall day, it was unusually warm. Eventually she joined Sandy and read for a couple hours, basking in the warm rays.

Then, growing restless, Karen put her book down. Going inside, she grabbed two ice-cold sodas. Handing one to Sandy as she walked back onto the deck, she asked, "What do you think about abortion?"

Startled, her friend glanced over at her. After a few moments of un-comfortable silence she responded. "I don't believe it matters what I think. You're the one who must live with whatever choice you make."

"I know. But if you were me, would you have one?"

Fidgeting with the plastic bottle, Sandy said hesitantly, "I probably would, although I know there is risk involved—physical complications as well as emotional issues."

"I've always thought of myself as 'Pro-Choice.'" Karen searched for the right words. "Yet now that I'm faced with this, I don't believe that abortion is the right choice for me."

"Oh?"

"Although I do admit it would solve most of my problems," Karen nodded as she spoke. "And certainly make Rick happy." She glanced at her friend to gauge her reaction.

"Yes, I worry about him. I've scheduled many concerts for him dur-ing the past two years, and I know how much his music means to him."

"True." Karen's eyes filled with tears. "His ministry is the main reason I struggle with what to do. I feel like there is so much more to consider than just the two of us—or should I say three?" The pain deepened in her chest as she wiped her eyes.

"He called me this week—after I spoke with you and learned what was going on. I've never heard him sound so scared." She caught herself. "Karen, I'm sorry. I shouldn't have said that. I'm here for you, to support you in whatever you decide."

"Thank you. I can't tell you how much I appreciate your friendship." Yet even as the words left her mouth she felt a vague sense of uneasiness, something she couldn't quite put her finger on.

The sound of a lobster boat in the harbor caught the women's atten-tion. They watched as the white boat, its paint peeling badly, halted a few hundred feet offshore from the cottage, and two men hoisted several large traps from the dark blue-gray water. They examined each lobster quickly, keeping the ones that met the regulation size and hurling the small ones back into the water.

"This is so interesting!" Sandy exclaimed before taking another sip from her drink, a gleam in her eyes. "Can you imagine living here year-round?"

"Yeah, Maine's a different world." Preoccupied with her thoughts, Karen looked at Sandy and forged ahead. "We've also discussed adoption. Got any thoughts on that subject?"

With a sigh Sandy leaned back in the lounge chair, gazing up at the sky. "If it were me, I know I couldn't do it."

Karen grimaced. "I don't know if I can either." She felt a strong pang of possessiveness. *My baby.*

"Why don't you keep it?" Sandy asked after a few minutes, still staring at the sky.

"I keep coming back to the conclusion that I can't afford to raise a child, or emotionally nurture a child, all by myself for 18 years." After another sip Karen set the bottle down beside her chair. "I'm still trying to get myself back together since my divorce, both emotionally and financially." She longed for words that would explain her innermost feelings—feelings that seemed logical to her but sounded strange when she said them aloud. "I've spent the past 17 years raising a wonderful daughter, but I don't want to start over again. It'd be too overwhelming to do it alone."

"Does that mean you've decided on adoption?" Sandy stared intently at her.

"Rick and I have talked about it several times, and most of what he says makes sense."

"What's his rationale?" Sandy shifted, leaning forward in her chair as she looked questioningly at her.

"He told me about his parents. About how they married and had him while they were only 17. His mother had the beginnings of a very successful career as a dancer, but had to give that up when she had him." Karen searched for words. "Rick has always believed that she resented him because he stood in the way of her career."

A stunned expression crossed Sandy's face. "Oh! I've never heard him talk about that."

Karen stared out at the ocean, barely able to make out where the water ended and the sky began. "Rick is convinced that I could do the very same thing—resent this baby if I were to keep her, because she would prevent me from reaching my professional goals."

"Do you think he's right?"

"I've thought about it, though I find myself questioning his motives for making that kind of a statement, since I know he feels threatened by all of this." Karen traced the outline of the arm of the chair with her index finger. "I'm not sure what to think. Maybe he's right." Was he though? Would she truly resent her own child? *Surely I'd love her . . .*

That night she lay in bed unable to sleep as countless thoughts flashed through her mind. It was a relief to be able to share her problem with someone other than Rick. However, that same uneasiness that she had felt earlier, something she couldn't put into words, now returned.

Back and forth, like the waves outside her window, her emotions fluctuated.

I'm thankful that Sandy is so supportive. Karen smiled in the darkness as she remembered the talks the two of them had had. Down deep she had no doubt that their friendship was genuine. But still there was that small, nagging sensation. After pulling the covers closer around her neck, Karen replayed Sandy's earlier comments about Rick again in her mind. *"Yes, I worry about him and his ministry . . . I've never heard him sound so scared."*

"So scared." Yes, it's obvious that she's worried about him. A second later a realization formed in her mind. *And torn between her friendship and loyalty to both Rick and to me!* Karen's heart sank as it all became clear.

She's known Rick much longer than she has me, Karen reminded herself, *so her loyalty to him is natural. Will she try to convince me to have an abortion too?*

I feel as if I have to watch what I say about Rick—that I can't let myself get too angry about him—for fear of offending her. She caught her breath again. *Or, worse yet, what if she were to tell him things that I say . . . or thoughts that I confide?* Now she had another worry to deal with. *Is there nobody I can truly confide in?* she wondered, feeling utterly lonely.

Exhausted from her emotional tug of war, Karen focused on the waves pounding outside of her window, blocking out everything else, until eventually she fell asleep.

WEEK 13

Karen carried the three bags of groceries through the kitchen door and placed them on the counter with a sigh. After a full day at work she had run several errands, eventually stopping by the market for groceries.

Relieved to be home after a long day, she quickly changed into comfortable clothes before returning to the kitchen to put away the food. Once she had donned her jeans and sweater and drew the blinds on her windows each evening, she could allow herself to relax and unwind. Her apartment had become a haven, a place that she longed to go to after the stress of work.

Opening the cupboard doors, she placed each item from the grocery bag into an exact spot, turning each label toward the front and lining the cans up perfectly. Perhaps she had been a grocery stock person in another life, she had once kidded with a friend who had teased her about her obsession.

Karen turned to make sure the outside door was locked after completing her task. Her heart jumped, and she caught her breath painfully as she noticed the big star marked on the calendar hanging beside the door. *I don't even want to think about that deadline!* she thought, her heart sinking.

Making her way to the couch, she wrestled with what she should do. *Once next Thursday passes, there's no turning back.* Two weeks ago she had telephoned a clinic to find out when the last possible day was that an abortion could be performed. Although they preferred to do them before 12 weeks, it could take place up until the fourteenth week, but dates had to be strictly confirmed by ultrasound. Next Thursday was it. After that, abortion would be ruled out. Deep down she knew it already had been, but it was comforting to know during her moments of panic that it was still a possibility. *What will I do when Thursday passes?* When I know there's no way out?

Karen prepared a salad and microwaved some leftovers for supper. Her mind repeatedly returned to the impending deadline. *I'll call Sandy tonight—to get some last minute advice.*

The woman had remained a source of encouragement. With a smile Karen reminisced about their trip to Maine the previous weekend. Having

Sandy to talk with, to bounce ideas off, had helped. As she heard herself verbalize the thoughts that had been floating through her mind, Karen felt increasingly more solid in her direction. Despite the subtle uneasiness as to whether she could trust the woman totally, she knew that Sandy cared and was a friend. And she was the only person Karen could talk to—and she needed someone. She would wait a bit and see how things developed, she had finally concluded on her trip home from Maine.

Several times throughout the evening she called Sandy but received no answer. Eventually, totally exhausted, Karen went to the bedroom and changed into her freshly laundered pink flannel pajamas. They felt soft and comforting against her skin. Once on her knees beside her bed Karen poured out her heart. "Dear God, how can I trust You enough to do this?" Her mind wrestled with making the final decision against abortion. "Do You understand what You are asking me to do? I will lose a career that means everything to me, and who knows how my friends and family will react." When her mind could not deal with it any longer, she got up off her knees and sank into bed.

Her thoughts returned to her life "before the news." Although it had only been three weeks, it now seemed like an eternity ago! Life had been so simple then. Karen wondered how she could have taken it for granted. Her concerns about what outfit to wear to what event and deadlines for small projects at work now paled in comparison.

After tossing and turning for almost an hour she jumped when the phone rang. "Hi, how are you doing?" Rick asked with little emotion.

"Another exhausting day. How 'bout you?"

"Same here. I'm not sleeping, missing appointments, and I've been forgetting the words to my songs in the middle of concerts." He took a deep breath. "Have you thought anymore about going to the clinic?"

"Yes, I've thought about it."

A long silence followed. She hoped he wouldn't push the subject tonight. "I'm going to bed—just wanted to check in with you," he finally said, his deep voice weary.

Rick had kept his promise to call each night. Sometimes she wished that he hadn't been so faithful, since because of his touring schedule he often phoned late. During each conversation the first week he brought up the topic of abortion, and Karen wondered if it was his way of wearing down her resolve. Eventually, she began to wonder if he had a heart at all. Lately, each conversation was tense as they each grew more withdrawn. *It feels like the last year of my marriage,* she realized. *As if we're just postponing the inevitable.*

Like every other night during the past three weeks, she had a hard time sleeping. And when she did, nightmares haunted her. A frequent dream involved the headline on the front of *Christian Contemporary Music* magazine. She saw a photo of Rick with a caption reading: "Christian Singer Fathers Child Out of Wedlock." Another reoccurring dream consisted of a conversation between Karen and her boss as he fired her from her job. Still other nightmares included family members as they responded in horror to the news.

Awakening with a start, Karen glanced at her clock—exactly midnight. She lay back down, but something felt strange. She paused. What was that feeling? The impulse to get out of bed almost overwhelmed her. Giving in to the strong urge, she slid from out under the covers and onto the cold floor. As she knelt on a small scatter rug that lay beside the bed, there wasn't much between her knees and the hardwood floors. Grabbing her pillow, she positioned it under her.

"Dear Father," she began, propping her head up with her folded hands. "I'm tired. I'm emotionally exhausted. I can't take this anymore." Tears filled her eyes and she paused. "Father, I believe that You have a purpose for my life. And somehow I believe that You have a resolution to this problem." She stopped, reflecting on how God had led her through her divorce, through her career path over the years, and in so many other ways. "I need an answer tonight, Lord. I can't go on any longer without hope." Despair consumed her. "I'm going to kneel here until You give me an answer." Her own words astounded her.

Wow, that was pretty bold, she admitted to herself, slightly nervous. *I hope He understands that I wasn't trying to be rude, just desperate in my need for answers.*

The night was still and the room warm. No noise came from her apartment building, which was unusual. Nor did the wind howl outside the windows. It was so silent that she could hear the beating of her heart as she knelt. A sense of awe crept through her as she felt the presence of God. A text flashed into her mind: "I will never leave you or forsake you." *I claim that promise, God. I won't let go of You. And You hold me, please. Tell me what to do! I need You, God! I can't do this alone!*

Waiting for answers, she shifted her weight from one knee to the other and longed for the comfort of her bed. Yet she was determined to remain on her knees until she received an answer.

In the night stillness a clear, single thought ran through her mind. **Do the right thing.** A moment later it repeated again: **Do the right thing.** And a third time: **Do the right thing.**

"OK, God, I will rule out abortion," she prayed aloud. "So I guess that means I'm committed to having this baby. But what now? Do I quit my job? Where do I go? What do I tell people?"

She waited for more answers. A few moments later another thought filled her mind. **I can shut their eyes.**

What does that mean? Her mind whirled as she tried to grasp each thought. Once again: **I can shut their eyes.**

I don't understand.

A third time: **I can shut their eyes.**

Karen remembered the story of Daniel and how God had shut the lion's mouths. *Is it sort of like that?*

She continued on her knees a little while longer. Nothing more came, only a peaceful feeling. *OK, that's a start, God,* she thought despite the fact that she didn't fully understand. Getting up off her knees she crawled into bed and fell back asleep.

Once again Karen could not take her eyes off the girl in her dream. Once more, she was sitting on a blanket in the park, dressed in a fresh green spring dress and white sandals. Her dark hair shone, highlighting a hint of natural curl. Magnificent brown eyes sparkled, dancing with excitement as she played with the golden retriever puppy. The puppy, licking her face playfully, frolicked around, and the child giggled as she rolled on the blanket. Unlike the first time she had this dream, Karen now saw the child's parents preparing their picnic lunch. Both were fair-haired, in stark contrast to the girl's dark features. They prayed with the girl before eating. The mother washed the girl's face immediately after the meal and brushed her hair again before she resumed playing with the puppy. *She's very well cared for,* Karen thought.

As she eased out of the dream, Karen felt an unexplained calm and was no longer nervous. *God, what are You trying to tell me?* It was 6:00 in the morning, yet she felt rested for the first time in several weeks. *It's going to be OK. Somehow it's going to turn out all right.*

WEEK 14

A tiny seed of faith had been planted the night that God spoke to Karen. She had begun to believe that He would work things out, although she still wasn't sure how.

However, those moments of hope and serenity shattered each evening when Rick telephoned. Listening to the growing fear in his voice made her chest tighten. A sickness would start in her stomach and grow until it reached her throat, leaving a bitter taste in her mouth. Every night was the same. This couldn't go on.

The emotional tug of war left her exhausted. One minute she felt her newfound faith growing inside her, and then the next Rick pressured her to have an abortion. And her faith alternated with apprehension. Although she believed that God would somehow get her through the crisis, she was uncertain about her future, acknowledging that she'd have to face the consequences of her actions—*their* actions—head on. And without Rick. *I'm not sure I have strength for this.*

When the walls of her apartment began to seem as suffocating as her problem, she knew she had to escape, if only temporarily. Throwing on a windbreaker, she drove to a nearby lake and parked along the shore. It was windy, and she stayed within the shelter of the car. She switched on the CD player and gazed out over the dark choppy waves to the low hills beyond, longing to be soothed by the music.

As she gazed into the cloudy sky above, she spoke quietly to God. "Dear Father, I ask You to speak to Rick. Soften his heart somehow." Pausing for a moment, her moist eyes focused on a cloud in the distance, she continued, "You know I can barely handle my own pain and problems, let alone his." Wiping her face with a tissue, she leaned the driver's seat back, reclining slightly, and closed her eyes. The song poured over her, easing a little of the anguish that tore at her heart. *There just has to be a way to take away this pain. There just has to be.*

Twenty minutes later she started the car and headed for home. She dreaded walking through that door, knowing that sooner or later Rick would call. As she pulled into her parking spot, Emily drove in and parked two spaces down. Karen's heart sank as she realized that her eyes were bloodshot, and she had no way of avoiding her friend.

After taking one look at her, Emily exploded. "What happened? What's wrong?"

Breaking down completely, Karen was unable to speak.

"You're in bad shape. Let me walk you to your apartment," Emily said. "You've been blaming your recent moodiness on your divorce, but you know, I'm not buying that anymore. What's really going on? Has Rick hurt you?"

The two women sat in Karen's living room. Emily, stubborn and protective, wasn't about to leave until she found out what had happened. And Karen, who was just as stubborn, knew that it was something that she must keep to herself. She still wasn't sure what the future held, or how or when she was going to deal with her pregnancy.

Eventually she regained her composure. "Emily, right now I can't talk about what's on my mind. I'm just trying to sort things out. I hope you'll understand."

Eventually the younger woman realized that Karen wasn't going to open up, no matter how much she begged. "OK, but I'm going to be checking on you tomorrow."

"We'll talk," Karen reassured her as she squeezed her friend's hand. "Just not right now."

After Emily left, Karen sat in the stillness of her apartment, overwhelmed by her situation. Pretending at work that all was fine was tiring, yet manageable. However, now she also had to conceal her pain from Emily, the person that she spent the most time with. She didn't dare confide in her and put her job at risk.

The telephone startled her. Instinctively she knew that it was Rick.

"Hello," she answered softly.

"How was your day?" His deep voice sounded weak.

"Rough. How about yours?"

He choked. "Karen, I can't stand this any longer." During the long silence she heard him sniffle. Although pain had become the trademark of his voice during the past few weeks, she'd never heard him sound so bad.

Her heart ached as she paced the floor. "I know." *I can't take it anymore, either!*

"This is the last possible week to go to the clinic. There's no more putting it off. Please . . ." His voice broke again.

Panic filled her, and out of nowhere she blurted, "OK, I'll go tomorrow."

Her words shocked both of them. Eventually he said, "Really?"

"Sure. Why not? What's the big deal?" she continued, not knowing if she was kidding or finally giving in. Her emotions ran the gamut: Anger because he wouldn't let up. Surprise, because she would give in to his pleading. Curiosity as to how she would feel if she began to question again whether she should or shouldn't have the abortion.

"Do you mean it?" he inquired cautiously.

"I might as well have one. You won't be happy until I do."

"No, I told you that I'd accept whatever decision you made."

"Well, you haven't! Otherwise you'd quit nagging me."

"OK. OK. Call me in the morning if you are serious about this."

"I will," she mumbled, exhausted once again. *I've got to get him off my back.*

Laying on the couch, deep in thought, Karen contemplated their conversation. *What would happen if I were to tell him that I had an abortion . . . yet didn't?* The thought intrigued her. *Finally, he would leave me alone. He could go back to his carefree life, singing as if he meant it again.* She knew that the past few weeks had taken a toll on his concert ministry. Totally preoccupied, he had forgotten the words to songs several times each evening. His manager had pressed him about what was wrong, but Rick had never acknowledged any problem.

Thou shall not bear false witness, a voice spoke quietly in her head.

Yes, I know, she conceded despondently. *But it would be so easy to get him to leave me alone this way. I really can't take his pressure any longer!*

God is our refuge and strength.

Karen knew that she needed to rely on God more, but wasn't exactly sure how. Having a strong independent streak, she prided herself in solving her own problems.

Exhausted, by 9:00 she had slipped into her pink flannel pajamas and knelt beside her bed. "Dear Father, please show me what to do. I can't handle Rick's pressure anymore." It felt as if a cement block sat on her chest, squeezing the breath out of her.

"I know it's wrong to lie." She struggled for the right words, pouring her heart out to God. "But unless You inspire me with a better idea, I'm going to call Rick in the morning and tell him that I'm having an abortion. I don't know what else to do."

Thou shall not bear false witness . . .

Overwhelmed, Karen didn't want to hear that voice again. She longed for a quick, easy solution.

Just as she was drifting off to sleep, the phone pierced the darkness again. Mumbling, she reached for it. *What does he want now? Can't he wait for morning to hear my answer?*

"Hi, Mom," came a familiar voice from the other end of the line.

"Sarah!" Karen was thrilled. "It's so great to hear your voice!" Glancing at the clock, she quickly counted five hours ahead to calculate the time in Europe. "What are you doing up at 2:00 in the morning?"

"I'm cramming for finals, but wanted to call you before going to bed. Got any plans for Christmas?" she began, then without waiting for a response, blurted, "I got a ticket to the states, and I'll be flying home to spend Christmas with you next week."

"Oh! Where'd you get the ticket?"

"Dad got it with his frequent-flier miles. I'll be with you for three days, including Christmas, then I'll go to Colorado to spend a couple more days with him."

"I'm so excited!" was all Karen could manage to say. And it was true—waves of excitement flowed through her at the thought of seeing her daughter after all these months. But sheer terror alternated with them as she wondered how to keep her condition from Sarah. Pretending at work, where she stayed in her office or was out often, was one thing. Being on the alert 24 hours a day around someone who knew her so well was another. Just the thought of keeping up a facade for several days running was exhausting. Sarah was certain to bring up the subject of Rick, most likely in the hope that she'd hear he was out of the picture.

"I'm so excited too, but I'd better get to bed if I'm going to pass my first final tomorrow. I'll e-mail you with the details. It won't be any problem to pick me up from the airport, will it?"

"Uh, no. Not at all. We'll be out of school by then too."

"Great. Look for a message tomorrow, if I'm awake enough to write. Love you."

"Love you, too, sweetheart."

"Gotta run. I'll see you next week."

Stunned, Karen sat in the darkness of her bedroom, propped up in her queen-sized bed, trying to wrap her mind around the brief conversation that she had just had. Having been so immersed in her struggle with Rick, it was difficult to switch gears and focus on this news. Next week was Christmas, and she had planned on doing nothing, since Sarah wouldn't be home. She wasn't in the mood for a celebration, that was for sure. But now her daughter was coming home, and she now had to prepare for the holiday.

It took Karen a long time to fall back asleep. The problem of whether or not to lie to Rick was now compounded by the new and additional pressure of her daughter's impending visit. Facing the extra task of making Christmas enjoyable and memorable for Sarah seemed like the last straw. *It's too much,* she wanted to scream. *Too much!*

Awaking every few hours, Karen slept restlessly. Finally she noticed dawn creeping in from between the blinds. Glancing at her clock, she noted that it was only a few minutes before 7:00, and the alarm would ring soon.

Flipping the alarm off, her mind began to whirl. *I've got to call Rick and get him to leave me alone.* The thought of honesty and relying on God drifted through her mind, but she quickly rejected it. *I can't take it anymore. Deceiving Rick is the only way,* she argued with her conscience. Her heart was heavy, for down deep she knew that she should be patient and let God work out her problem. Yet she felt pushed to the edge of an emotional precipice, and she was determined not to go over it. She would put an end to this today.

Karen rubbed her eyes and propped both pillows beneath her head. *Here goes nothing,* she thought as she dialed his number.

"Hello," a sleepy voice mumbled at the other end of the line.

"Aren't you awake yet?" she played, stalling.

"I'm trying."

"I'm taking the day off and going to the clinic." She tried hard to sound convincing.

"Really?" Excitement replaced the sleepiness.

"Yes, really. So now you don't have to worry about this anymore."

"Who will take you?" he asked nervously.

"I'll drive myself. When I spoke with the woman at the clinic she said that I could stay there for most of the day until the anesthetic wears off," Karen answered uncomfortably.

"Well, OK." He paused, unsure of what to say next. "I'll call you tonight to check on you and make sure you're all right."

After saying goodbye, Karen showered and prepared for work. She hated the thought of lying to him. However, if she could get him off her back and allow him to return to a normal life, it would let her focus on her mission to survive the ordeal and to find a good home for her baby.

The day dragged on forever. All morning she attempted to concentrate on a presentation that she was preparing. Her heart wasn't in it, however, and creativity was hard to muster. She knew that she was wrong—that lying wasn't the answer. As she restlessly straightened papers on her desk, her heart seemed heavier than ever.

After lunch Jenni hurried into the office. Before Karen could say hello, the girl plopped down into a chair. "I'm so mad at my parents!" she blurted. "They don't understand anything!"

Karen got up from her desk and went to sit beside her. "What's happened with your parents?" She gave the girl a hug.

"They want me to go to one college, and I want to go to another," Jenni began, wiping her eyes. "They think I chose the college that I want because Josh is going there."

"Did you?" Karen asked cautiously.

"No!" Jenni was defensive. "Well, at least not totally. I mean, of course I want to be with Josh, but I want to go there anyway." She growled. "They make me so mad! I wonder if my real parents would be this way?"

Stunned, Karen wondered what she hid behind her phrase "my real parents"? Attempting to maintain her composure, she inquired, "What do you mean?"

"I'm adopted," Jenni stated matter-of-factly. "They finally told me last summer—after all these years."

Taken aback, Karen knew she must focus on Jenni's problem, not her own. "What do you think your birth parents are like?"

At first the girl didn't know how to respond. "I think they'd be cool, and they'd trust my judgment on matters like this." She smiled, gazing out the window as if worlds away.

"Well, love is wanting what's best for someone. You've told me enough about your parents that I am confident that they desire the best college for you. I'm sure of that."

"Yeah, I know," Jenni conceded. "It's just . . . I'm so frustrated."

Karen wrapped her arm around the student and squeezed her. "Why don't you go home and ask your parents why they want one college instead of another. Let them explain their reasoning and at least be patient and listen."

"OK," Jenni agreed sheepishly. "I didn't really give them a chance to explain."

"Well, try it and see how you feel afterward."

"Yes, Ma'am." Jenni grinned at her. "I need to finish a paper before class this afternoon." The girl stood and grabbed her book bag. "Thanks for listening."

Sitting back in her swivel chair, Karen was soon lost in thought. She enjoyed her interaction with students. And she had never before spoken with someone adopted. Intrigued, she vowed to have further conversations with Jenni in hopes of gaining a better understanding of adoption from a child's perspective.

After work, Karen prepared fettuccine Alfredo and a salad for supper. It was rare that she cooked. Usually she just had a prepackaged meal via the microwave. However, all afternoon she had craved Italian cuisine and had purchased the fresh ingredients on her way home. Just as she was about to place the noodles in the boiling pot of water, someone knocked at the door.

"Emily!" she exclaimed as she opened it. "Come in."

"I'm here to check on you, to see if you're doing better than yesterday." Emily wandered into the kitchen, taking a seat at the table while Karen continued to prepare her meal.

"I'm fine." Karen smiled, deliberately acting cheerful as she dumped the noodles in.

"Does this have anything to do with Rick? Has he hurt you?" Emily demanded, not convinced by her friend's attempt to pretend that all was fine. "Because if so . . . ." Her dark eyes became fierce.

Karen stirred the noodles without making eye contact. The comment about Rick hurting her had struck a nerve, and she was fighting hard not to cry. "I have a problem that I can't talk about right now. I need to figure it out myself before discussing it."

"Why can't you tell me? I'm one of your best friends."

"I need to think through this more—before we chat."

"Why do you always have to think through everything before talking?" Emily rarely thought before she spoke. Her openness, Karen had often thought, was one of her most endearing qualities as well as one of her biggest weaknesses.

"Listen, don't worry. When you get back from your trip over Christmas we'll talk," Karen promised, wanting to buy some time.

"Well, if you're sure." Emily glanced at her watch. "I've got to get home. The kids have probably killed Grant by now. I'll see you when we get back." The two friends hugged before Emily bounded out the door.

What am I going to tell her? Karen wondered as she drained the noodles and put the finishing touches on her meal. *She knows something's wrong. Don't worry about that now, though,* she reminded herself. *Remember: one thing at a time. I've postponed that conversation till after Christmas.* As she devoured her meal, Karen mentally switched gears and began thinking about her impending phone conversation with Rick later that evening.

At exactly 6:00 the phone rang. It was the call she had dreaded all day.

"How'd it go?" His voice was shaky.

"I don't remember a thing," Karen began, winging it.

"Do you regret doing it?" he asked hesitantly. "I mean, are you OK with everything?"

"Too early to tell," Karen dodged, feeling disgusted at misleading him. "How do you feel?"

He sighed. "Relief, mostly. I worry about you, though. I don't want this to traumatize you." After a short pause he repeated, "I'm just relieved that it's over."

Her emotions exploded, like a soft drink bottle that someone had shaken and then opened. "How can you take this so lightly?" she ripped into him. "This is a baby we're talking about—a real person—and you don't have any regrets about killing it?" Tears flooded down her cheeks. *How could I have ever loved you? Don't you have a heart in there anywhere?* She placed her hand on her stomach and caressed it gently, relieved that she had not let him really talk her into an abortion.

"Have you told Sandy yet?"

"No. I don't feel like talking to anyone right now. Please call and tell her."

"Sure."

Karen lay on the couch and sobbed for a long time after hanging up the phone. She had hoped that she would feel relief now, since Rick would no longer be pressuring her. Yet she was consumed with guilt for lying and ashamed that she had insisted on her own way, demanding that God solve problems on her timeline and not His. And when He hadn't, she had gone ahead with her own plan.

For a moment, she thought of the biblical account of King David and his tendency to fix his own problems instead of letting God intervene. Yet despite all of that, the Lord had still called him a man after his own heart. Somehow comforted, she wiped at her tears.

An overwhelming need for forgiveness engulfed her. Kneeling in the stillness of her apartment, she pleaded, *I'm so sorry, God. I'm confident that You've already forgiven me for my original sin, because Rick and I prayed together for that. But tonight I ask You to forgive me for lying to him. And please forgive my lack of faith—for not having faith enough to wait on Your plan.*

WEEK 15

Christmas music blared from the public address system in the Wal-Mart as Karen wandered aimlessly through the aisles. Apparently others had also put off their holiday shopping and now were frantically trying to find just the right item for each person on their gift list. After searching through the clothes section for a present for Sarah, Karen headed toward the music and electronics section in hopes of seeing something that appealed to her there.

I'm not in the mood for Christmas this year: I don't have any desire to sing or be merry. Nor do I have the energy to wrap presents. And I sure don't want to have to be on guard during my few days of vacation, worrying that Sarah will discover that I'm pregnant. Although she felt guilty for her thoughts, she couldn't help but wish that her daughter would remain in Europe this Christmas.

A newborn's cry pierced her thoughts. For an instant Karen squeezed her eyes shut in pain, then reopened them quickly as she realized that she had strolled into the newborn section on her way to the CDs. Racks of pinks and blues and yellows and greens surrounded her. Everywhere she looked she saw infant clothes, blankets, and accessories. Suddenly feeling claustrophobic, she searched frantically for a way out of the department. Gazing to her left she spied a very pregnant woman with a tall man beside her, leisurely looking at baby clothes. Instinctively Karen looked for wedding rings. Yes, the couple had them. No doubt they were happily married, longing for the soon arrival of their little one.

Karen recognized that she had nothing in common with that other woman: *I'm not happy, certainly not married, and not eagerly anticipating the birth of my baby.* More pain welled up in her as she fought her way to the aisle, seeking to get as far away from the infants department as she could.

She struggled for control of her emotions. *Calm down. When I get home I've got to begin thinking about avoiding situations like this. Being around baby clothes, pregnant women, and newborns are things I can't handle anymore.*

Approaching a rack of CDs, she slowly flipped through selection after selection. *Country? No, I don't think Sarah's into that.* Moving down a few steps, she gazed at the pop CDs. *This isn't it, either.* Eventually she gave up in frustration. *I don't know what Sarah would like! She's a teenager, and her tastes change daily.*

On the way to the door, a row of picture frames caught her eye. Sarah had become interested in photography after arriving in England. Fumbling through a shelf crowded with every style of frame imaginable, Karen found one that particularly interested her. It had several styles of cutouts, from ovals, to squares, to octagons, and would hold 10 photographs. The frame had a rich looking gold trim with shadows of black. Karen smiled at her find. *She'll love this! Now I must find wrapping paper and bows.*

The radio was on when she turned the ignition switch in the car. More Christmas music. Irritated, she punched it off. Under a tremendous amount of pressure as she faced an uncertain future, she now had the additional responsibility of trying to make a memorable holiday for Sarah.

Gritting her teeth, she thought, *Just do it and get it done. Get through it.*

Once home, Karen attempted to relax by watching television as she wrapped her daughter's presents. In addition to the frame, she had purchased a few practical items as well—toothpaste, deodorant, a couple phone cards, and a package of peppermints, Sarah's favorite candy. *This way, she'll have several items to open on Christmas morning,* Karen thought as she finished taping the last package.

A knock on the door startled her. *Who could it be this evening? Please not Emily,* she hoped, reaching for the knob. *I can't handle anymore questions.*

"Hi, Ms. Williams," came a chorus of voices. Three students stood at the door, grinning boldly as they handed cards to her. Final exams had ended, and almost everyone had left campus for the holiday.

"Come in!" she beckoned. "Why haven't you all gone home yet?"

Jenni, Amber, and Julie burst through the door into the living room. "We're just getting ready to leave," Jenni began. "Amber's mom is driving us, but we wanted to bring you a card and wish you a Merry Christmas." Each girl hugged Karen.

"Hey, where's your tree?" Amber asked curiously as she gazed around the living room.

"Yeah, aren't you excited about Christmas?" Julie piped in. "I can't wait to get home and help my mom decorate our tree."

Karen paused. "I've been so busy with school that I haven't had time. But Sarah's coming home now, and I'll get the tree up before she arrives." She hoped she sounded convincing.

A horn honked, and the girls took their cue to leave, each hugging her one more time on their way out the door. *They are great kids!* She had formed bonds with several of the students and enjoyed the times that they would drop by her office and chat. *What will they think when . . . ?* She forced herself not to think about it.

The phone rang as she shut the door. *Now who is it?* She didn't want to talk with anyone. "Hello."

"Hi, how are you doing?" Rick's voice reflected his new lease on life. Ever since he believed that she had gone through with the abortion, he had sounded like a different person.

"I'm tired, but fine. Sarah's flying home for Christmas, and I'm trying to get things ready for her."

"Oh? You must be excited."

"Yes," Karen mumbled half-heartedly. "But I have so much to do before she arrives tomorrow."

"I'm going to my parents' house for Christmas," Rick said. "My dad's not been feeling well, and I want to spend a couple days with them. Thought I'd let you know where I am in case you need anything."

"Will you stop by here on your way through?" Karen didn't know if she wanted to see him or not. His parents lived about an hour away.

"I was thinking about it, but I'm not sure."

"Well, have a good Christmas."

"I will. Say hi to Sarah for me. Bye."

Karen's thoughts flashed back to when she had first told her daughter that she was dating him. It had been a difficult conversation for both. Although Sarah was not a child, her parents' divorce had hurt her, and she had never felt comfortable around Rick. "I can't put my finger on it, but I just don't like him," she had remarked to her mother. "I don't think he likes children." Karen now laughed bitterly. *If you only knew.*

Again, the phone rang, startling her. *Who is it now?* she wondered again. "Hello."

"Hi, Karen." Sandy sounded perky on the other end. "Merry Christmas a couple days early."

"Thanks, you too!" Again Karen worked to sound upbeat.

"How are you holding up?" Sandy asked nervously. "I've been thinking of you a lot since Rick called." She paused. "I was surprised. I thought you were considering adoption."

"Yeah, I was, but, well you know," Karen said, fumbling for what to say. She had put off calling her friend, not wanting to lie to her also.

"Well, I don't mean to pry. Just wanted you to know I'm here if you need to talk. I'm sure it's not easy right now, with Christmas and all."

"I appreciate your friendship." Karen's voice broke with emotion. She wanted to come clean, to tell her everything. But that small, nagging feeling lingered, and it kept her from blurting out the truth. If she confided in Sandy, would she tell Rick? She couldn't take the chance. *I am so tired of always being on guard, of having to weigh every word!*

"I've got a party to go to, so I must cut this short. But I wanted to wish you a merry Christmas."

"You too. I'll call you next week."

Eventually the phone stopping ringing, and Karen opened the card the girls had given her. "Merry Christmas!" it shouted at her with its red and green construction paper letters. They had made it themselves. Inside each girl had written a message. "Thanks for listening," Jenni's flowing handwriting said. "It means a lot." Karen smiled. *My work matters,* she reminded herself. It was one of the reasons why she loved her job. Unlike the teachers, who had to be concerned about grades and essay deadlines, she could just talk to the students and offer advice. Her heart raced at the thought of losing her job. *What will Jenni think?*

The next afternoon Karen paced back and forth inside the airport terminal, full of nervous energy. She had prepared as much as she could for Sarah's arrival—the apartment was clean, she had wrapped the presents, she had planned for the next couple days, and she had even managed to decorate a tree despite the fact that she wasn't in the mood. Strangely enough, having a goal—preparing for Sarah's visit—had given her something to focus on and allowed her to relax a little.

A woman's voice boomed on the public address system, drowning out the chatter in the terminal. "Flight 2056 from New York City will arrive at Gate 16 in five minutes." That was Sarah's connecting flight. Karen's heart fluttered. She pulled her coat tighter, paranoid about what lay beneath her black, flowered sweater. Attempting to ease her fear, she reminded herself that she wasn't showing yet. *And besides, a pregnancy is the last thing that Sarah would ever suspect or be looking for!*

Face after face passed by as she anxiously watched for her daughter. Blond hair . . . was it her? As the girl drew near Karen recognized the smile. "Sarah!" They embraced tightly. "I can't believe you're really here!" She hadn't realized how much she had missed her daughter.

Together they walked to the car and chattered the entire way home. Sarah bubbled about her schoolwork, her friends, and the frequent sightseeing trips she was privileged to take as part of the foreign exchange student program.

As they neared the apartment, the girl asked cautiously, "Is Rick going to be around for Christmas?"

"I don't know, honey. We aren't planning anything, but there's a chance he'll stop by."

"Why aren't you two spending Christmas together?" Sarah asked curiously. "Are you still seeing each other?"

"We're just taking a break right now," her mother began, unsure of how to explain where their relationship was at. Her thoughts rambled . . . *Well, I'm pregnant, he thinks I've had an abortion, we're not getting along . . .* She dreaded the time when she'd have to tell her daughter the truth.

"What's his problem?" Sarah sighed and rolled her eyes. Then with a worried look she continued, "He hasn't hurt you, broken your heart or anything, has he?" Before giving her mother a chance to respond, she blurted. "He strikes me as the kind that, when the going got tough, wouldn't stick around."

Tears welled in Karen's eyes as the truth plunged like a knife deep into her heart. *If only she knew how close to the truth she was.* "Don't worry," she said, trying to sound convincing and reaching over to pat Sarah's hand, "I'm fine."

"I wish you'd find another man," the girl said with distaste. "He's not good enough for you."

Fortunately, at that moment they drove into the driveway, and her mother didn't have to respond.

They spent the evening unpacking and relaxing. Since it was Christmas Eve, a variety of Christmas classics were on television. After several programs, Karen yawned for the umpteenth time and announced, "You can stay up as long as you want, but I've got to get some sleep." She hugged her daughter goodnight and fled to the safety of her room, where she instantly fell asleep from exhaustion.

The next morning Sarah's voice awakened her. Just as she had done as a child, the girl was kneeling on her mother's bed, bouncing up and down and squealing, "It's Christmas morning. Wake up. Let's open presents."

Rubbing her eyes, Karen sat up and attempted a smile. "OK, OK. I'm on my way." Putting on her matching silk robe over her purple silk pajamas, she tied it loosely. Then, catching herself, she quickly unfastened the belt and let the robe hang. No need to draw attention to her waistline. Karen ran her fingers through her hair and followed Sarah to the living room. "May I take a shower first?" she asked, even though she already knew what the answer would be.

"Of course not! I can't wait another minute," Sarah said with a grin that melted her mother's heart. The two of them sat on the floor in front of the artificial tree. Small white lights flickered on and off. Hand-painted bulbs hung from the dark-green branches. A few cherished heirlooms had been clipped on toward the top. Sarah eyed every present carefully, taking her time, as she searched for the most enticing one to open first. After choosing, she gleefully tore at the wrapping, throwing the bow in the air and shredding the paper in her haste to get to its contents.

Her mind leaping back 16 years to Sarah's first Christmas, Karen remembered that even as an infant her daughter had opened her presents with the same intensity as she did now. Karen's eyes filled with tears as she envisioned Sarah again as a baby. Babies and Christmas . . .

"Mom." The girl's voice whisked her back to the present. "Are you OK?"

Her mother quickly wiped her eyes. "Yes, I'm fine." Attempting a smile, she prompted, "Keep opening. You have several more to go."

Each time that her daughter ripped open a gift, throwing the bow into the air and shredding the paper, Karen returned to that morning so many years ago. No matter how hard she fought the tears they always returned.

When Sarah finished opening her presents, she reached under the couch and pulled out a small wrapped box with a miniature bow on top. Handing it to her mother, she hugged her and said, "I could only get you one thing. Hope you like it."

"Oh, honey, you didn't have to. You can't afford to do this," she replied, unwrapping it carefully. "It's beautiful!" she exclaimed as she held up the gold, oval-shaped locket. Inside was a picture of Sarah.

"I found it in a shop in Paris a few weeks ago and thought of you."

"It's perfect. Thank you so much." Wiping her eyes with a tissue, Karen joked, "Now, you clean up the mess while I take my shower."

Getting up from the floor, she escaped to the safety of the bathroom. As the hot water blasted her skin, she sobbed. Memories of Sarah flashed through her mind. Ripping open each present on her first Christmas. Her first birthday, with chocolate frosting smeared all over her face as she grinned from ear to ear at the camera. The girl's first day of school, when Karen had cried, and Sarah hadn't.

The pain was intense, almost smothering Karen. *How can I even consider giving this baby up for adoption?* She held her stomach as the thought echoed through her mind. *I'll miss all of the firsts in her life, all of the memories.* Desperately she wished her mind would stop. *Maybe I'll find a way to raise her myself.* It was all too confusing, too complicated. Sobs wracked her body again. Eventually, she shut off the water and tried to pull herself together. Reminding herself that she didn't have to have all of the answers today, that she just had to get through the next few hours for Sarah, she finished drying her hair. *One step at a time . . .* That little but reassuring phrase had become her mantra.

Later that morning they sat down for their traditional Christmas video marathon. Barely making it through the first one without breaking down, Karen slipped into the kitchen to prepare Christmas dinner. Splashing some cold water on her eyes, she tried to keep the tears at bay. *I am so tired of Christmas! It's all about love, and families, and—children.* She dabbed the corners of her eyes with a paper towel. *I feel so alone and overwhelmed.*

"Hey, Mom, whatever you're cooking smells great," Sarah yelled. Several days earlier Karen had attempted to sit down and plan a meal. In frustration she had realized that her mind was paralyzed, still in a crisis mode, and that she was unable to handle even the most basic chores. The previous day she had gone to the deli and ordered food for two. Well, at least she could solve the meal dilemma, thanks to the deli.

"Time to eat," Karen announced as she straightened her china goblet, filled with a mixture of ginger ale and cranberry juice, to make the table setting perfect. She had set blue and white china plates for two and properly placed the silverware. A large vanilla candle burned in the middle of the table, surrounded by overflowing serving bowls.

"Wow," her daughter exclaimed as she entered the room. "Everything looks great!"

As they ate, Sarah kept the conversation going. Karen listened and commented, but was relieved that the girl did most of the talking, as her own mind wandered continually. Suddenly a lull came in the conversation. Sarah fiddled with her fork. Finally she blurted, "Mom, it's so weird not having Dad here."

Karen didn't know what to say. It was their first Christmas since the divorce. "I know," was all she could muster.

"Do you miss Dad too?" Sarah asked sadly, sounding like a child again.

"Yes, I do. But it was his decision to leave, and now we have to get on with our lives."

"I'm sorry. This holiday must be very hard for you," Sarah commented, suddenly sounding wise beyond her years.

"It's the saddest holiday I've ever experienced," her mother confided, being more honest than Sarah realized. Smiling as best she could, Karen continued, "But you are here, and we can have a wonderful time, so go finish your video while I clear the table."

Washing the dishes slowly, Karen savored the moments she had to be alone. Every task was such a chore—a conscious effort—and it was emotionally draining.

Startled by a knock, Karen whirled around. Before she could take three steps, the door burst open and a booming voice announced, "Merry Christmas. Anyone home?"

"Rick!" She hugged him tightly as he entered with a present in each hand. He looked good, dressed sharp for the occasion. As she gazed into his eyes she saw a rested and more peaceful look than she'd seen in some time. It confirmed her hunch. Deceiving him had allowed him to get back to his music ministry and a normal life.

Suddenly panicking, Karen quickly retreated to the kitchen. *Oh my, now I've got a second person that I must be on my guard around.* Her heart raced, and she felt her face flush. Desperately she sought a diversion, a reason to stall before walking into the living room and being with Rick and Sarah. As she reached for a glass and poured a drink of water, the thoughts continued. *All right, calm down . . . You aren't showing yet . . . True, you can't snap or zip your jeans anymore, but your sweater covers that, so calm down . . . Take a deep breath . . . There, now walk into the living room with a smile and pretend that everything's fine. You can do it.*

Forcing a smile, she went to the couch, propping a pillow from it discreetly in her lap.

"Hey pip-squeak, here's something for you," Rick said as he handed Sarah a small package. She smiled and sat up in her chair, tearing the paper off in two seconds flat. "Thanks," she said dutifully as she pulled a book out of the paper. *How to Visit Europe on $30 a Day.* Curiosity won out over her dislike for him, and she browsed each page with interest.

"Open yours," Rick said to Karen as he sat beside her on the couch. Removing the paper gently, she pulled out a video of her favorite southern gospel group. "Thanks! I love it."

They stared at each other for a second, uncertain what to say next. Karen could sense an undefined tension. Both of them were good at pretending that everything was fine, yet she knew that their carefree friendship had died the day that she had told him that she was pregnant. Now all that was left was pain and guilt. *We've ruined everything,* she thought with sadness. *Nothing will ever be the same again.*

Standing up, Rick nervously announced, "I've got to get over to my cousin Patty's house and see more relatives. Bye." He hugged Karen once more and hurried out.

The mother and daughter watched a string of Christmas videos throughout the afternoon. It was one of Sarah's favorite Christmas traditions, and Karen wasn't about to ruin it for her. However, during any scenes involving babies or pregnant women, she slipped out of the room.

The next morning she drove her daughter back to the airport to catch her flight to Colorado. Just before the girl went through security, the two embraced. "I love you. It's been so nice to have you home for a few days," Karen said. "E-mail me when you get to your dad's place."

"I love you, Mom. Take care."

As Karen watched the plane taxi down the runway and turn out of sight, she offered up a silent prayer. *Thank You, Lord, for helping me through these past couple days.*

Once inside her car at the parking garage, she breathed a sigh of relief. She had made it—had accomplished her goal of having a special Christmas for her daughter. *With Sarah gone and Rick off my back, I can finally concentrate on me. I can put all of my energy into dealing with this baby.*

WEEK 16

Glancing at her watch, Karen panicked. *Wow, I'd better get moving if I'm going to make it to my doctor's appointment on time!* It had been more than a month since her first visit, and after Sarah had left she had made her first official pre-natal appointment.

Back into her routine at work, Karen was thankful for the diversions each day brought. The constant challenges of her job distracted her from the issues at home. But each evening she had to refocus on making arrangements for her baby. It was her mission now, her special project. Thinking of it in those terms made it easier for her to deal with. It provided a sense of direction.

After straightening her desk quickly, she hurried down the hallway and left for her doctor's appointment in town. It was usually a 15-minute drive, but fresh snowfall covered the roads, and she drove cautiously.

"Karen," the nurse called. For an instant she again relived the terror, panic, and uncertainty of her first visit, and her heart raced at the memory. But as she began to walk down that same hallway, she soon felt more at ease.

Within minutes the doctor hurried in. Looking at her chart, then into her face, he had a puzzled expression. "I guess I'm surprised to see you today."

She nodded and smiled. Perhaps she was a little surprised herself. "Yes." She stared at the floor. "It's been a long month. Many sleepless nights." Her legs dangled off the table. "But I've decided to have the baby."

"You sound better than the last time we spoke. Lay down. Let's listen for its heartbeat and then measure your stomach."

The doctor placed the small black device on her belly and a fast *swish, swish, swish* filled the room. "The baby has a strong heartbeat," he confirmed. Instinctively, a smile spread over Karen's face. *Wow, she's really in there.* Remembering her first doctor's visit when pregnant with Sarah, she had been so eager to hear the heartbeat. Now she felt a growing excitement once again.

However, within moments, she fought the feeling. *I shouldn't be excited about this pregnancy!* Karen argued to herself, attempting to convince her head to override her heart. Yet, picturing the 1-year-old girl from her dream, her magnificent eyes beaming, she couldn't help but smile again. *I already love her.*

"Are you OK?" Dr. Jacobson questioned. "You seem preoccupied."

Wiping her eyes with the back of her hand, she said, "I'm confused, not sure what I should be feeling right now."

Next, the doctor placed the measuring tape on her stomach. "Right on target for growth." As she sat up he glanced at her chart. "I see you've lost weight. Have you been sick?"

"No, I've been lucky and haven't had morning sickness. I've changed my diet, though, trying to eat more balanced meals."

"But you shouldn't be losing weight."

"I'm not dieting," she protested. "I'm just eating healthy."

"OK, but by next month I want to see you put on some weight." He grinned.

That evening, lying in bed, Karen placed her hands on her expanding stomach. "I think I'll call you Sweetie," she said aloud. Replaying the *swish, swish, swish* sound again in her mind, she smiled and continued, "I heard your heartbeat today, and you sound spunky."

Her thoughts jumped around. *Pregnancy is supposed to be a time of joy, for sharing with someone you love. But here I am, alone and abandoned. Obviously Rick didn't love me as much as I loved him.* Her heart felt like a lump of lead. *Another man I've loved and lost.*

The following evening she went to Grant and Emily's house for supper and to catch up on everything that had happened during Christmas vacation. They had been gone for two weeks, visiting family in Florida, and had invited her for a home-cooked meal.

"Come on in," Grant welcomed as she removed her coat and boots. "Emily's in the kitchen. Go on in."

The smell of sautéing onions beckoned Karen toward the kitchen. "Hi, Emily, how was your Christmas?" she asked, pulling up a stool and making herself comfortable.

Emily, dressed in her usual comfortable attire of jeans and a sweater, stood in front of the stove, putting the final touches on the evening's meal. "We had fun—for the most part. But Christmas in Florida is weird—no snow, and just warm weather. I'm glad to be back home," she commented as she poured the gravy into a bowl and then headed toward the table with the remainder of the food. "Let's eat," she called to her husband and kids.

After saying grace and serving the children, Emily turned toward Karen and asked, "So how are you doing now? You weren't very happy the last time I saw you."

"I'm better."

Emily took one glance at her face. "I don't think I believe you. Try again."

Karen's mind scrambled, attempting to come up with something to pacify Emily. "Rick and I seem to be drawing apart right now," she began, telling the truth, yet leaving much unsaid. "For now we are just going to take some time, think about our relationship, and see where it goes from here."

"I'm glad," the other woman replied, wiping her mouth with her napkin. "You know I don't like him, and that I think you'd be much better off without him."

"I know." Working to steer the conversation in another direction, Karen said, "This roast is delicious. I wish you'd cook for me every day."

Much to Karen's relief, the children had finished with their meal and begged to leave, providing a welcome distraction.

After clearing the table, the two women sat in the living room chatting about Christmas. Upstairs they could hear the noises of the children playing. Emily sighed. "It's so exhausting sometimes," she confided. "I'm looking forward to when they'll be older, and I can go back to work." She laughed. "Work I actually get paid for!"

"Is it worth it, staying at home to raise them?" Karen asked, curious.

"Definitely." Emily looked fondly at the doll on the couch next to her. "It's so tiring at times, but I wouldn't trade these years for anything. Seeing the first steps, watching them play, being able to teach them about Jesus . . . I wouldn't have it any other way. And Grant is so supportive," she bragged. "He takes them when I need time off."

A barrage of emotions surged through Karen—fear that she would begin crying in front of Emily, and anger that Rick didn't love her so that they could be celebrating their baby's impending birth. As she struggled to remain composed, she searched for an excuse to depart immediately. *I've got to get out of here!* She feared that she would hyperventilate.

"You know, Katie was an 'accident,'" Emily rattled on. "We only wanted three kids." She shook her head. "I was devastated when I found out I was pregnant. It was just so stressful already with three, and I was just starting to lose all those extra pounds, and here I was pregnant again." Without waiting for Karen to respond, she went on. "Not that there was anything we could do about it though, so we just decided to make the best of it. But before too long we fell in love with her, even though she hadn't been born yet, and now our family just wouldn't be complete without that baby."

Karen felt tears coming. *Think of something funny,* she told herself.

Just then the telephone rang and after a moment Emily mouthed the words, "It's my mom." Knowing that it would be a lengthy conversation, Karen stood. "I'll catch up with you tomorrow," she said as she opened the front door and hurried out into the cool evening air. As she walked through the darkness toward her apartment, she let the tears flow freely. *How will I ever find the strength to keep up this charade?*

Karen spent the next two evenings scouring the Internet for information on adoption. Sifting through site after site, she read about the many different options. Unlike years ago, when adoptions had been closed and very secretive, birth mothers and adoptive parents could now tailor their specific desires into formal agreements and end up with anything that both parties agreed upon. Frequently, adoptive parents shared in the delivery experience and had considerable contact with the birth mother after that. *If I do this—really go through with an adoption—I would want to decide what I am and am not comfortable with.* Her mind raced with ideas, yet ultimately it left her sad at the prospect of giving up her child.

One website particularly caught her attention, and she returned to it repeatedly for more information. It was a licensed agency, only a couple states away from hers, and had been in business for many years. Also it was a Christian organization. Jotting down the phone number, Karen stuck it on her computer. *One of these days I'll call.*

All week Karen stared at the number, attempting to get up her nerve to phone. Each time she began putting questions together in preparation for the call, she would burst into tears and put off the task until the next day. *Tomorrow I'll do it,* she promised herself. *Tomorrow.*

Finally, late one afternoon, she decided that she could stall no more. Nervously yanking the number off the computer, she reached for the telephone and sat down on the couch. Slowly she punched in the number. Her chest rose and fell with each breath and her mouth became dry. When she tried to clear her throat, only a faint squeak came out. She hung up quickly as huge tears rolled down her cheeks.

"I can't do this! I just can't!" she exclaimed aloud as she threw the phone down on the couch next to her. *I'm calling someone about giving away part of myself!* After a few minutes she managed to pull herself together and dialed the number once again . . . slowly . . . more fear arising with each number. Again, she couldn't breathe. Again, no words came out. As she heard the phone ring a second time, she hung up, tormented by the pain in her chest.

I don't want to do this! I shouldn't have to do this! Pulling her knees up in front of her on the couch, she wrapped her arms around them tightly. *Why? Why? Why?*

Perhaps adoption wasn't what she should do, she second guessed, stalling. Lying back on the couch she reviewed how she had arrived at her decision. *Down deep, I know it's right.* She had spent many hours thinking and making lists in an attempt to work methodically through her situation.

Adoption is best for the baby, she began going down the list in her mind. *She deserves a loving home with two parents that want her.* Karen knew that adoptive parents often waited many years for a baby and had no doubt that her child would be loved and wanted. *But I love and want her,* a voice nagged inside her.

I don't have the energy or the financial resources to raise her all by myself at my age. She had no one to rely on financially. Sooner or later, whether or not she placed the baby for adoption, she knew that she would lose her job once people found out that she was pregnant. Already she had begun sending out résumés in an attempt to locate another position before getting fired. However, even if she was fortunate enough to transition into something else, she still wouldn't be able to support herself and provide for Sarah, plus pay for daycare and the other expenses that would accompany a newborn baby. As it was she was barely making ends meet on her present salary.

And the dream. Karen had also replayed the dream many times in her mind. *About a year old . . . Her dark hair shone . . . Magnificent brown eyes sparkled . . . The child's parents preparing the picnic lunch . . . Both were fair-haired, in stark contrast to the girl's dark features . . .* Through the dream, Karen believed, God must be confirming her choice of adoption.

As she lay on the couch, replaying the reasons that she had chosen it, she prayed. *Dear Father, please give me strength to make this phone call. It's so hard. I believe that it's right, but my heart just breaks each time I try. Help me God, please. I need You.* Sitting up, she reached for the phone and dialed. Although she was still nervous, a new inner peace and strength grew by the minute. *I am not alone.*

WEEK 18

Large snowflakes floated to the ground outside the window. Sitting at her impeccably neat wooden desk in her office, Karen was deep in thought, putting the final touches on an upcoming presentation.

During the past few weeks she had settled back into a relatively predictable routine at work. Through prayer and meditation she had put much time and thought into various strategies for surviving her ordeal. Time management was one key element, as was her goal to keep her two worlds as separate as possible. When she walked into her office at 8:00 each morning she diligently focused on work, exercising her willpower more each day as distractions and panic plagued her. And likewise, after arriving home, she focused on her "second job"—planning her future and finding a home for her baby.

As a guidance counselor, her job included a variety of tasks. In addition to counseling students on everything from career choices to interpersonal relationships, she was also responsible for scheduling and overseeing all scholastic testing. Once a month she also gave a presentation against alcohol and drugs at small elementary schools throughout the state. Since she was fortunate not to have had morning sickness, Karen had been able to continue with her travel schedule.

A loud buzzing jarred her from her thoughts. "Line one is for you," the receptionist announced.

"This is Karen. May I help you?" She held the receiver to her left ear as she leaned back in the blue swivel chair, crossing her legs.

"Hello," came a broken voice. It took her a few seconds to realize that it was Rick.

"What's wrong?" she panicked, sitting upright.

"My dad passed away this morning."

"Oh, Rick! I'm sorry." She caught her breath. "How are you holding up?"

"We knew it was coming," he sighed. "I'm more worried about my mom."

"When's the funeral?" Karen doodled with a pen and paper in front of her.

"Saturday, in our home church. Will you . . . Can you make it?" he asked nervously.

"Sure."

After she hung up she felt her heart start to pound. She stood and began pacing, frantic thoughts bombarding her. *What am I going to wear?* At work she had been wearing sweaters and dress pants with elastic in the waist, and so far they were working fine. *But I don't have anything dressy enough to wear to a funeral.*

What am I going to wear? she wondered again, placing her hands on her growing abdomen. Quickly she jerked them away, glancing at the doorway, hoping that no one had seen her. Karen had worked at trying to avoid such gestures. A few weeks earlier she had sat in church and observed a pregnant woman. Studying her movements, the way the woman placed her hands on her protruding stomach, and her lumbering waddle, she had noted the typical body language of an expectant mother. She mentally vowed to pay close attention and consciously to avoid anything that would give away her secret. Only in the safety of her apartment, during her nightly talks with her unborn child, would she allow herself to place her hands on her stomach and let her guard down.

Throughout the afternoon Karen's mind kept returning to the subject of clothing. As hard as she tried to refocus on her project, panic continued to win out, and her mind wandered. Picturing her closet, she mentally took inventory. *No, the navy dress is getting tight—that wouldn't work.* She had a favorite dark green pantsuit, but the top wasn't long enough to camouflage her midriff. *I will go to the mall after work tonight,* she concluded. *Hey, this could be fun,* she tried to tell herself, remembering how she had used to love to shop for clothing. She couldn't quite convince herself, however. What if she couldn't find anything suitable?

The class bell rang and within a minute Jenni popped into Karen's office and slumped down into a chair. "Got a minute to talk?" she asked in a frustrated tone.

"Sure."

"I'm still arguing with my parents about this college thing," she began, shifting her book bag from her lap to the floor. "They just don't understand."

"Jenni," Karen interrupted, "did you talk with them about their reasons for wanting you to attend the other college?"

"Yes. They said it's better academically, as well as being closer to home. They want me to be able to come home frequently on weekends." The girl sighed heavily.

"Those are good reasons, Jenni. Have you given them any thought?"

"Yes, some. But I want to pick which college I attend. They frustrate me so much!"

"Do you think the real reason you're upset with your parents is because they didn't tell you that you were adopted until recently?"

Puzzled, Jenni sat quietly, deep in thought. "Well, yeah, that does still bother me, but . . ."

"Do you think that college isn't the biggest issue between you and them?"

"I don't know. Maybe. It's not like it would have made any difference if they had told me sooner. I guess it's just that I feel as if I have been lied to for most of my life."

"Tell me more. Do you think that they don't love you? Would you have wanted to know about being adopted earlier in life?" Karen leaned back in her chair, attempting to act relaxed, yet the fluttering of her heart increased. She longed to learn more. *How does an adopted child feel? How do the adoptive parents treat them? How do . . .*

"I know my parents love me. But I wish they'd told me from the start. I'm not sure why they didn't." The girl shrugged, looking at her. "I mean, I guess it would be hard for them to tell me, but I don't know why. I'm actually interested in finding out about my biological parents though. I mean, I'll always think of Mom and Dad as my parents, but it would be kinda cool to meet my birth parents. Just to see what they're like. Although that could be awkward too," she sighed. *Jenni's just rambling,* Karen thought. *She's confused.*

The two chatted for almost 30 minutes, mostly about Jenni being adopted, though occasionally about other topics, as well. Eventually the bell rang again, and the girl stood. "Thanks for listening. I'm going to be late for class! See you later!"

As Jenni rushed out the door, Karen's thoughts continued to whirl. *She seems to be well-adjusted. She knows she's loved. She only wishes she'd known earlier. That's understandable. I wonder if she'll find her birth parents.* Her mind leaped to 20 years in the future and the possibility of meeting a young woman who looked like her. The thought made her heart sink. *Maybe it'd be better if Jenni doesn't find them.* But she was curious to know more about what it was like to be an adopted child. As she returned to her project, Karen looked forward to her next conversation with Jenni.

The snow had stopped by mid-afternoon, and the stars shone brightly as she pulled into the parking lot at the mall. It was only 6:00, yet it was dark. Karen despised this time of year, when the sun set each evening around the same time that she got out of work. Pulling the collar of her blue coat up around her neck, she shivered as she hurried into the mall, stomping the snow off her boots once inside.

Walking through the door of her favorite store, Karen breathed a prayer for just the right outfit. She loved to shop and could browse for hours, but this time she was on a mission and managed to remain focused on her goal. *It needs to be a dark color, since it is for a funeral.* She continued down her mental checklist. *I want something professional, since I'll have more public appearances related to my job in the future.* Searching through row after row of skirts, blouses, and dresses, she found only two outfits to try on.

The first was a navy dress. Gazing into the full-length mirror, Karen cringed at the unflattering way it looked on her. Although it was expensive, with white and navy trim around the collar, it just hung there without form. *I look like a tent,* she thought with a grin.

The second option was a dark green skirt with an antique white lacy blouse. Karen had never worn skirts and blouses since they didn't flatter her body. However, in her quest for clothes to hide her pregnancy, she had decided to lay aside all preconceived ideas regarding clothing and try a variety of styles to determine what would and wouldn't work. *This is definitely not right for hiding a pregnancy,* she acknowledged as she observed the way they accentuated her stomach.

Disappointed, she put the items back on the rack and made her way to a nearby restroom, closing the door behind her. *Dear God, I really need something to wear. I know this sounds like a vain request, but You've made a promise to me, and now I need the right clothes to hide my pregnancy.*

Wandering back into the store Karen rummaged through a few more racks. Eventually she spied a long row of suits hanging against a side wall. She hadn't considered suits, as they were usually formfitting, but something drew her to the rack. As she searched for her size, her eye caught a black suit with stylish white trim down the front. Lifting the hanger from the rack, she turned it around, smiled, and then headed to the dressing room.

It fit perfectly. The white trim provided a tailored look, actually adding a slenderizing effect. The suit included both a skirt and dress pants, each with an elastic waist. Karen turned from side to side. Nothing showed. She looked thinner in the suit than she had in months. *Dear God, You're amazing!* What an answer to prayer!

As Friday evening approached Karen began to get nervous about the funeral the following day. Attempting to keep occupied, she cleaned her apartment thoroughly. Once she had completed that, she picked up a book and settled on the couch to read, but soon she was on her feet again, pacing, her mind awhirl.

I'll call Sandy, she thought, reaching for the phone. Soon a soft voice answered.

"Hi, Sandy. How are you?"

"Oh, Karen, I was going to call and check on you this evening. Perfect timing!"

"You are always checking on me. Thought I'd call you this time." Karen appreciated Sandy. Although the woman had no idea what was really going on, their friendship had continued to grow, and she called Karen regularly to chat and encourage her.

"So, how's the job search going? I still don't know why you want to leave your job at the school."

"I keep sending out résumés, but I'm not getting any response. I've always been able to land a job easily, so this is frustrating."

"Well, stay where you're at. You like working with the kids, and it's a good job."

"I know." It would have been nice to tell her the truth. But something held her back. Could she trust her not to tell Rick? *I can't take that chance,* Karen reminded herself once again.

"Not to change the subject or anything, but I assume you're attending the funeral tomorrow?"

"Yes," Karen sighed. "I'm not looking forward to it." Avoiding the real reason why she was hesitant, she continued, "I liked his dad very much. It'll be an emotionally draining day."

"Rick is glad that you're going to be there. Your support means a lot to him."

Anger flared in her. *I wish he had been supportive of me in my crisis! But everything is always about him.* She despised his selfishness. The main reason that she had agreed to attend the funeral was to be supportive of his mother and to show his father respect. Otherwise, she would have thought twice before going.

"Well, Sandy, it's late, and I'm tired. I just wanted to check on you for once and see how you are," Karen concluded wearily.

"Thanks for checking. Take care."

As Karen knelt beside her bed that evening, she prayed specifically for Rick and his family. Then she crawled between the freshly laundered sheets and pulled them up around her neck. Repeating what had become her nightly routine, she placed her hands on her stomach and spoke quietly to her unborn child. "Hey, how's it going in there?" She smiled in the darkness. "Tomorrow is going to be a rough day. I have to go to your grandfather's funeral." Karen was quiet for a minute. "You would have liked him."

Saturday morning Karen awoke with butterflies in her stomach. She hadn't seen Rick for three weeks and was now concerned about her growing girth. He was observant when it came to women and their clothing. While she wanted to be supportive of him and his family during their time of grief, still, emotionally drained herself, she wasn't sure what to say or do.

Her hair was a mess, and her eyes weren't fully open as she slowly stumbled to the kitchen. Opening the refrigerator door she searched for something special for breakfast. Comfort food. Yes, that was what she needed. Not much of a breakfast person, she had frequently skipped it altogether in the past. However, realizing that proper nutrition was important now, she had begun eating a high protein breakfast and had been pleased with the results. Not only had she found her concentration greatly improved at work and her moods more even, but she had even lost a little weight.

Pulling out a small non-stick skillet, she prepared a cheese and mushroom omelet. As she waited for the frying pan to reach the right temperature, she cracked two brown eggs into a bowl. Adding a small amount of milk, a pinch of salt, and a mixture of Italian seasonings, she beat them together with a large silver whisk. She'd never been much of a cook, but this was the one thing that Rick had taught her to make. Grating a little extra cheese, she dropped a few shreds into her mouth and then placed the rest inside the omelet along with a handful of mushrooms.

Carrying a blue-and-white china plate in one hand and a glass of orange juice in the other, she went to the living room and sat down on the couch. As she ate, her mind went back to the first time she had watched Rick make breakfast. Karen had invited five students to her apartment for lunch one day, after they had helped her complete a difficult project at work. She had teased them, bragging that she'd have a gourmet chef cook them lunch. At first, Rick's suggestion of a multi-course lunch with breakfast foods surprised her, but she agreed, knowing that whatever he fixed would be good.

Karen knew that she was going to enjoy the meal when her nose caught the first whiffs of his cooking. He stood at the gas stove, skillfully working two large skillets. In one he had fried potatoes and onions sizzling, flooding the apartment with a rich aroma. The second held a large yellow omelet, bursting with colors protruding from every side—small diced green and red peppers, white onions that had become almost transparent as they tenderized, large brown mushrooms, and golden cheese oozing out the side.

Her mouth watered as she gazed at the large fruit salad sitting on the kitchen table in a chiseled glass bowl. It held whole red strawberries, large blueberries, diced kiwi, slices of orange, and star shaped cubes of fresh pineapple. *Wow, when Rick makes a meal, he does it right!*

While he cooked, Rick bantered with Mike, one of the male students. They had taken an instant liking to each other. Watching the two together, Karen wondered if the boy reminded him of his own son, who would be close to the student's age. Rick rarely spoke of his son, and when he did, Karen sensed the topic was painful.

When she glanced down at her plate, she saw that it was empty, not even a crumb remaining. As she carefully placed her dishes in the sink, she sadly concluded, *I really miss those good times with Rick.*

After showering she dressed for the funeral. Nervously she checked her suit several times in the full-length mirror, scrutinizing herself from head to toe and from every angle. *I guess I'm as ready as I'll ever be.*

When she pulled into the driveway of the traditional stone and wood church she looked for an empty parking space. A fluffy layer of fresh snow covered the ground, giving everything a clean look. She smiled to herself as she remembered the first time that she had attended there with Rick. It had also been the first time she had met his parents.

Once inside the church she immediately spotted him, talking with some people in the foyer. Nervously, she pulled her coat together. Within a few minutes he noticed her and made his way over.

"Glad you could come." His voice echoed sadness, and his eyes were dull with grief. "May I take your coat?"

Hesitantly, she slipped it off and handed it to him, her heart racing. She longed to put the coat back on, to hide beneath it throughout the service. *No,* she reassured herself, *I must believe that this suit looks good and that no one will notice a thing. Be confident!*

He gave her the once-over. "You look radiant," he commented. Scanning her from head to toe again he continued, "There's something about you today . . ."

Frightened that he'd discover her secret, she excused herself as other people approached him and slipped into the sanctuary. *If you only knew why I look radiant!*

Finding a pew near the back, she straightened her jacket, making sure that it was not too snug. Placing her purse on her lap, she rested her arms across the purse, letting them further camouflage her stomach. She glanced around to see who was there. Mr. Davidson had been loved and respected, and the church was packed. Rick's mom sat quietly on the front row, along with his siblings.

As Karen waited for the service to begin, she observed the people as they flooded in, hugging each other and offering words of encouragement. Up toward the front she spied Patty, Rick's cousin, whom she had met several times before. It was she and her husband that Karen had thought about as adoptive parents for the baby. Patty was dressed in a navy dress with matching hose and shoes. She always had her hair styled in a fashionable way. Wondering about her age, Karen guessed that she was in her mid-30s. *They would be great parents for the baby,* she thought again. *Could that be God's plan?*

The service included several music selections, a statement to Rick's family's love for and involvement with music. Rick's mother enjoyed the old hymns, and she dabbed her eyes with a white lacy handkerchief while a family friend sang her husband's favorite.

As Rick walked to the platform to deliver the eulogy, Karen's heart flip-flopped. Dressed in a sharp black suit, a starched white shirt, and an elegant gray silk tie, he commanded attention as he nervously placed his notes on the podium. Although he was a seasoned performer, she still felt concerned for him. This had to be the hardest thing that he'd ever done.

In the beginning his voice was monotone as he presented the formal information—date of birth, residence, and date of death. As he got further along in the speech, he shared the fun and humorous side of his father. At each of the funny points he would pause, look up, and break into a subtle smile. The audience began to chuckle.

Karen listened carefully to each comment, yearning to learn more about his father, a man that she had only met a handful of times during the past year. As Rick described his father's sense of humor, his love for friends and family, and his commitment to his church, she realized that he truly had been a wonderful man.

Rick's next statement took her by surprise. "My father loved children, especially babies." For the first time during the eulogy his voice broke. Struggling for composure, he refused to give in to emotion.

As Karen wiped her eyes with a tissue, she wondered what Rick must have been thinking when he wrote that sentence. He believed that she had gone through with an abortion, and had no idea that she was still pregnant. *Is he feeling guilt? Has he stopped to wonder how his father would have reacted to that kind of choice? What would his father have thought about becoming a grandfather again?*

Fellowship and refreshments followed the service. Mourners gathered in a large meeting room attached to the church. Large scrapbooks lined a long table draped in a blue linen tablecloth. The books showcased many events in Rick's father's life. Karen flipped through the pages, searching for photos of Rick as a child. Suddenly she felt uneasy. Glancing to her left, she caught him watching her intently. Realizing that he had a full side view of her, her heart raced, and she turned quickly the other direction. In a moment he made his way to her side.

"There's something about you today," he commented. As she looked up into his dark brown eyes, Karen recognized the exhausted and painful look she had seen several weeks before. She wondered if he would have been able to handle the stress of her pregnancy and the death of his father at the same time. Her hunch was that it would have been too much.

Rick reached for her elbow. "Thanks for coming today, but I need to get back to my family. I'll call you later, and maybe we can get together before I leave for home."

After saying goodbye to Rick's mother and a few other people, Karen put on her coat and began the trip home. "Thank You, God, for getting me through this," she prayed aloud. Although she wasn't sure what the future held, she was glad that under her black suit, the symbol of mourning and death, there grew a new life.

WEEK 20

Full of anticipation, Karen awoke before the alarm clock could ring that Friday morning. She had the day off and was heading down to visit Sandy for the weekend. For the past couple weeks the trip had provided something to look forward to. But mixed in with her excitement she also felt a sense of anxiety. Hiding her pregnancy over the phone was one thing—would she be able to keep it a secret when she was actually in the same house as her friend?

Within an hour Karen had showered, dressed, packed, and was loading her small overnight bag into the car. *I hope I've remembered everything.* It would be a casual weekend, and she was only taking a couple sweaters in addition to her small leather bag. Grabbing three more CDs, she closed the door behind her.

All that Karen saw during the first hour of her trip were back country roads that wound through farm country, up large hills and down through picturesque valleys. Despite the fact that it was winter in New England the sun was shining and good weather was predicted for the weekend. Sunshine glistened off the snow as it lay in the surrounding fields. Many trees still cradled patches of snow on their branches. Karen surmised that once she got three to four hours south, she wouldn't see snow anymore, and that was a welcome thought.

Listening to Christian music as she drove, Karen bathed in the peace and serenity that it brought. She also prayed frequently throughout the trip, expressing her thankfulness for the chance to get away for a few days and avoid the pressures that were mounting in the community where she lived and worked. "Thank You, God, for getting me this far," she said out loud. "I'm trusting in You to get me all the way through this."

She would face only one pressure this weekend—keeping her secret. But that didn't concern her too greatly, however, since her stomach hadn't grown much, and she had brought several loose fitting outfits. Her theory was that people in general, if they weren't looking for something, could easily overlook what seemed obvious to her. Still, she was slightly worried. Surely Sandy wouldn't be looking—or would she? Karen's heart fluttered with nervousness.

She made good time on the trip, and her only stops were to use the bathroom. It was the one true hint of her condition, and it continued to get more bothersome as time went by.

As she pulled into Sandy's driveway, she glanced at the surrounding houses. *This is the kind of community that I'd like to live in.* Each house was relatively new and appeared to be well built in a variety of contemporary styles, their lawns meticulously taken care of. It was a nice change from her apartment and its surrounding buildings.

Before she could get out of her car, Sandy drove in next to her. "I hope you haven't been waiting long," she said as she got out. "I've been rushing around getting my errands done, trying to get last minute groceries for the weekend." She smiled. "I'm so glad you're here."

"Oh, I just arrived. May I help carry some of your bags?"

"Sure," Sandy responded with a smile as they went inside.

After putting the groceries away Sandy changed into comfortable clothes while Karen took her small overnight bag and hanging clothes to the guest room. Glancing around, she saw that the room was just how she had remembered it from her first trip with Rick. A sharp pain went through her as she remembered the happy times with him, before all this had happened. *I feel so abandoned,* she thought. But no sense in letting her mind go there. She had come here to enjoy the weekend. Forget Rick. She returned to the living room.

"Well," Sandy began as she sat down on the couch for a minute. "What do you think of the idea of going out to dinner and relaxing over a good meal before we head over to the concert tonight?"

"Sounds like a plan. Italian or Mexican?" Karen asked with a smile. They had discovered that they both had the same two favorite kinds of foods.

"Italian," Sandy smiled. "Let me get my jacket, and we can head into town now so that we will have plenty of time." "I'll drive and you can relax," she added as they got into her blue minivan. For a moment Karen panicked as she wondered what to do about the seat belt. If it was too tight it might reveal her secret. Pointing out the window, she asked a question about a nearby house in an attempt to keep Sandy preoccupied while she fastened the belt, adjusting it to make a looser fit, and hoping that her light jacket would camouflage the rest. Karen mentally congratulated herself on her strategy. *It's almost like a game.*

While her friend drove, Karen enjoyed the scenery. Sandy lived within 10 minutes of a large metropolitan city, and the area was very different than what Karen was used to. She glanced at the tall buildings and was enthralled with the shops and miles of storefronts. *Maybe I'll find a job in a place like this,* she thought, getting rather excited. Perhaps leaving her current job and starting over wouldn't be so bad. *I could get used to this.*

Within 20 minutes they arrived at a nice Italian restaurant and were seated. Once they had placed their orders, Sandy remained quiet, a questioning look on her face. Karen was about to say something when the other woman began, "Tell me the truth. How are you doing? I've been worried about you ever since you had the procedure done."

Karen caught her breath. It was the moment she knew had been coming. *Don't ruin it now,* she told herself. Playing with her drinking straw and avoiding eye contact, she replied, "I'm OK. Some days are better than others, but I think I'll come out on the other end." There. It was a factual answer, although she knew it was misleading. *I'm not lying, exactly.* She tried to ignore the frustration she felt building inside her. *I don't want to spend the weekend discussing this. I want to forget about it!*

Sandy took a sip of her soda, "Do you regret what you did?"

After a long contemplative pause Karen answered honestly, "No, I don't regret the decision that I made." There. Another truthful statement. *Stop asking questions,* she pleaded silently.

Before Karen could figure out how to change the subject Sandy broke the silence. "Well, let's not talk about this anymore. I just wanted to make sure you're all right. Since you had asked my opinion before you had it done, I didn't want you to have regrets or be upset at me." Her eyes had a serious, thoughtful look to them.

So Sandy's feeling guilty! "Let's just enjoy the weekend," Karen said with as much of a smile as she could muster. "Don't worry about it." *Yeah, don't worry about it.* She wanted to roll her eyes. *If only I could stop worrying about it.*

After a leisurely dinner and conversation about work, children, and Rick, the two headed across town to attend the Christian concert that was the focal point of their weekend. They enjoyed all kinds of music, and Sandy always scoured the local papers looking for concerts coming to the area. One of their favorite groups was performing in concert at a local non-denominational church, and they wanted to get there early to get good seats down front.

In the lobby Karen noticed a sign that listed 2,013 as the occupancy rate. *Wow, it didn't look that big from the outside.* Inside the sanctuary had four large sections of pews covered with comfortable blue-gray cushions. Heavy wooden beams that ran from the peaked ceiling down to the floor accented the white walls. Large windows filled the space between the wood beams on each side wall. A semi-circle platform encompassed the entire front wall and was two steps up from the main floor.

As they entered the sanctuary sound check was just ending, an indication that they were almost an hour early. They sat on the second row directly in front of the platform. A moment later two of the four-member contemporary quartet sauntered down from the stage and stopped to greet them, shaking hands and chatting for a few minutes before heading to the bus to change.

Sandy beamed as she turned to Karen. "This is so much fun. Thanks for coming down."

Karen was smiling too. "My pleasure. I needed a break."

By 7:00 the church was packed, and the concert got off to an ener-getic start as the group began with their latest hit. Their harmonies were tight, and the sound system delivered an impeccable mix, much to Karen's delight. She had a critical ear for music that was not mixed properly.

Each person in the group shared short testimonies, allowing the audi-ence to get familiar with them, and many of the comments were exactly what Karen needed to hear. Music was the most effective means of wor-ship for her. *God, You are so wonderful,* she prayed silently. *You've given me assurance of Your leading. Please continue to guide me.*

Following a couple of quieter ballads the group began an up-tempo song. When the music started, Karen felt a steady kicking within her ab-domen. Instinctively her hand moved toward her stomach, but she caught herself. *I can't give away my secret,* she thought, silently speaking to her baby. *Hello there, Sweetie! You like the music too!* She felt her eyes growing moist. If only Rick could know about this, if only he could feel his child respond-ing to the music he loved. Then she sighed. *I want to tell someone!* Karen almost turned toward Sandy to share her news, then caught herself at the last minute and realized that she couldn't say a word. *I guess it's just between you and me, Sweetie. But I feel you! I know you're there!*

It's as if she reacting directly to the music. During the next song, which was a ballad, the kicking subsided and Karen began to recognize a pattern. *You're a little drummer!* By now she was so excited she had a hard time con-centrating on the music.

During intermission Sandy turned to her and exclaimed, "They are so good! I'm glad you could come down for the weekend." Although Karen smiled and nodded, she was too preoccupied to think of a good response. *Hopefully Sandy doesn't think I'm acting strange,* she worried.

Soon the second portion of the concert began, and once again Karen became lost in her thoughts, grateful that she had an excuse to not talk with Sandy.

The concert ended late, and Karen was unusually quiet on the trip home. "Are you OK?" Sandy asked, concern evident in her voice.

"Yes, I'm fine. I guess I'm just really tired!" She forced a laugh. "I need to get to bed, I suppose." Sandy nodded, but Karen thought she still looked worried. *Oh well, I'm doing the best I can.* Once she was safely in her room and in bed, she finally allowed herself to give in to her emotion, crying softly for a long time. Placing her hands on her midriff, she wondered, *How will I ever be able to give you up?*

Her thoughts kept returning to the concert that evening and the distinct reaction that her child had each time she heard a strong rhythm. She flashed back to the time when she was pregnant with Sarah many years before and had attended a country music concert. Even then, at a time that was much later in the pregnancy, Sarah did not respond in the same way that Karen had felt this evening.

This baby has two major music influences in her life, and she will be musically talented, was the thought that ran through her mind as clearly as if someone was speaking to her. She wanted to call Rick, but she knew she couldn't. *He wouldn't care.* Bitterness seeped into her mind. *He doesn't want her.*

Eventually she dozed, but soon awakened again from the need to use the bathroom. Irritated, she got up and struggled to find her way to the door in the darkness. *I forgot how annoying this was,* she grumbled to herself.

At breakfast the next morning Karen sat at the table, fumbling with her French toast and fruit, wishing for several more hours of sleep. As she got up from the table to pour herself a glass of juice Sandy looked at her, gazing from head to toe with a puzzled look on her face. Feeling self-conscious all of a sudden, Karen turned her back to Sandy and attempted to maneuver back to the table without revealing too much of her profile. But before she could think of anything to keep the conversation light Sandy said, "Karen, I heard you getting up to go to the bathroom three times last night. Is everything all right?"

"I must have drank too much before going to bed," was her feeble excuse.

"If I didn't know any better, I would think maybe there's more to it than you are letting on." She searched her friend's face for a reaction.

"What does that mean?" Karen replied, her heart racing fiercely. *Did Sandy know?*

"I don't know. I guess I shouldn't make assumptions that I can't back up." She began gathering the dishes while Karen went up to shower, dress, and pack for her return trip that afternoon.

In the shower Karen mentally reviewed the tasks that awaited her once she arrived home. She needed to complete the adoption paperwork, but had kept stalling, not having the heart to finish. Suddenly she remembered a section of the paperwork requiring the birth mother to indicate criteria that she desired in adoptive parents. She had already decided that she would request that the adoptive parents be Christians, but other than that she had not given it much thought. As long as they wanted a baby, had the money to support one, and would love the child, that was all that had seemed to matter.

Once again the thought was clear in her mind. *This baby has two major music influences in its life, and she will be musically talented.* Perhaps she should request that the adoptive parents be actively involved in music so as to cultivate and nurture her child's talent. A smile crossed Karen's face and a peace filled her heart. *Thank You, Lord, for continuing to guide me through this process,* she prayed as she shut off the water and prepared for her day.

WEEK 22

Karen stared out the icy window in her office. Snowflakes swirled down in a never-ending spiral. Sighing, she turned away and wondered how many days it had been since she'd last seen sunshine.

For the second day in a row she sat frustrated at her desk, struggling to schedule work-related trips. Once a month she traveled to small elementary schools around the state to present lectures against drugs and alcohol. Since such small schools didn't have budgets for guidance counselors, the principals and students always appreciated her programs.

Dates had been set for the visits several months ago. However, when she looked at her year-at-a-glance calendar on her wall, she panicked, noting all of the trips that she would have to make during the last couple months of the school year. She had begun giving serious thought to requesting a leave-of-absence at that time, fearful that she would be starting to show by then. *What am I going to do about all of those appointments?*

Mr. Harrington, the principal, interrupted her thoughts as he popped his head in the door. "Karen, the school board is meeting today, and they've just asked for a brief summary from each department. I know it's short notice," he said breathlessly. "Could you have something ready in 20 minutes?"

"Sure." Panic washed over her as her boss headed down the hallway. *I don't want to stand in front of the board members now. What if they notice my growing belly?*

She reached for a notebook in which she kept test schedules and results. *I can pull some good news out of here,* she thought, attempting to be optimistic. *I'll make this report short and only focus on the positive.*

After gathering the test score summaries, she stood up, brushed off her dress pants, smoothed her navy sweater, and took a deep breath. *I should go use the ladies room before heading down to the meeting.* As she walked up the hallway, Karen was convinced that she would wear out the carpet between her office and the bathroom. Entering the brightly lit lounge, she could hear the voices of several teenage girls.

"I'm sure she's pregnant," one girl chattered loudly behind one of the stall doors.

"Makes sense," another girl chimed in. "She's been acting funny, and she wears loose-fitting clothes."

Karen's eyes widened, and she stopped in mid-stride, shocked at what she had just heard. *Oh my! They've figured it out!* Her thoughts were racing as wildly as her heart. *What am I going to do?*

Another girl continued, "Well, Mrs. Rollins has been married for almost four years now, so it's natural that they'd be ready to have a baby."

"Yeah, both Mrs. Rollins and Mrs. Billings are that age, and I bet they'll each be making announcements soon," one of the girls bragged confidently as she opened the stall door and walked to the sink and turned on the water. "Oh, hi, Ms. Williams," she greeted Karen, and then chattered on.

Caught off guard, Karen tried to act relaxed and casual as the girls gathered around the sink and continued gossiping. Grateful for the empty stalls, she made her way quickly inside the nearest one and locked the door behind her. Closing her eyes, she sighed heavily, attempting to calm her racing heart. She was relieved that they hadn't been talking about her, and that they had actually been exchanging speculation on two of the younger faculty members with no children as of yet.

Only after Karen heard the women's room door open and close did she dare come out of her hideout. In the stillness of the bathroom, as she washed her hands and straightened her hair in the mirror, she realized in amazement, *Here I am, five months pregnant, and nobody has noticed. Yet these girls are keeping an eagle-eyed watch on two younger faculty members, wanting to be the first to confirm when they become pregnant. Since I'm older and divorced, they aren't even thinking about that possibility with me.* She smiled. *Thank You, Lord, for "shutting their eyes."*

Gathering her papers from the desk, she headed toward the conference room. She didn't have to wait long. A moment after she took her seat around the large wooden table the principal called her name. Thankful that she wasn't required to stand, she held her head high and spoke, feeling a warm peace fill her body. Board members smiled and appeared pleased that the school was on-target and, in some cases, above the national average in test scores.

Relief surged through her on the way back to her office. Collapsing into her chair she sighed heavily. *Thanks for getting me through, Lord. I don't have the strength for days like today.*

Later that evening she began aimlessly flipping through the channels on the television, hoping for something to help her relax. She was tenser than she had been in a long time. In addition to challenges with her schedule at work, there were also growing stresses with Rick. The occasional telephone calls were no problem. However, she worried how much longer she could keep her secret from him.

Restless, she changed positions, her mind wandering as she scanned the stations one more time. Suddenly, gripped by what she saw on *The Learning Channel,* she froze, fear surging throughout her. Painful memories flashed within her mind. On the screen was a woman giving birth, screaming in agony.

Quickly she changed the channel as a nauseating feeling swept over her. Her breathing became irregular, and her chest rose and fell sharply. Flashing back to Sarah's birth, she relived those agonizing memories, which she had long forgotten after gazing into her daughter's face. Karen's labor had lasted almost 20 hours and, even with medication, was excruciating and exhausting. Horrified, she sat on the couch, consumed by fear. It had just hit her that, like it or not, this was where her choice was leading her. And this time she'd be doing it alone. She wanted to scream, to unzip her body somehow, step outside, and run away.

Badly shaken, she walked slowly to the kitchen. A pan of brownies beckoned her from the counter. Smiling, she remembered the times that Rick had made brownies, then had put them in a bowl, scooped berry ice cream on top, and finished by adding Spanish peanuts and chocolate syrup. How she missed those carefree times when they had talked and laughed for hours!

Startled by the ringing of the phone, Karen returned to reality. "Hello."

"Hi, Karen," Sandy asked. "How was your day?"

Sitting on the couch sideways, Karen propped a pillow behind her back and stretched her legs out fully on the cushions in front of her. "All right."

"Wow, that didn't sound very convincing. What's wrong?"

"Nothing." She froze, searching for an answer. "I just have a lot going on at work."

"What's happened?"

"It's the time of year when I finish planning my spring schedule. There are a lot of presentations to fit in, and . . . well," she paused, "sometimes things don't gel just like I'd like them to." She hoped that sounded reasonable, knowing that she couldn't explain how the thought of standing in front of a room full of elementary students and their teachers, while concealing a pregnancy, was her primary concern. Fortunately, at her current job she was able to work in her back corner office. However, during her trips all eyes would be on her.

Sandy's voice was reassuring. "It'll work out. Don't worry so much." Before Karen could comment, she continued, "How's Sarah?"

Smiling proudly, Karen replied, "She's great. Really doing well with her studies and has made many nice friends."

"Wonderful!"

"How are Aubrey and Dan?"

Sandy bubbled, "Doing great this year. I don't see them much, since they're so involved with activities at school."

"That's a good thing, though."

"Yeah, you're right. Have you spoken with Rick lately?" Sandy's voice had a note of nervousness.

"Yes, he calls every week or two. Nothing is the same with us anymore, and I miss the old him." She paused and sadly commented, "I think he calls out of duty or something."

Karen heard a clicking on the line. "I've got another call coming in," Sandy explained. "Do you want to hold on a second?"

"No, I'll call you later in the week."

"OK, bye."

As she hung up Karen sighed. At least Sandy hadn't asked any difficult questions! Later she sat down at her computer desk to check her e-mail and to send a quick note to Sarah. She was thankful for the service as it allowed them to communicate frequently without having to pay expensive phone bills. Sure enough, she had a long note from Sarah, rambling on about her schoolwork and her friends. This time she mentioned a new friend. A boyfriend. Surprised, Karen smiled to herself. *Yeah, I guess I'd better get used to this, for she's that age.* Her mind wandered as she sat at the desk. *How am I ever going to tell Sarah that I'm pregnant? Sooner or later, I'm going to have to tell her.* Heart heavy, she hoped that her daughter would not make the mistake that she had.

Crawling into bed she snuggled down and stretched. Then, placing her hands on her stomach as she did each evening, she spoke quietly to her baby. *Hey there, you've sure been moving around a lot today, especially when I was so upset. Do you get happy when I'm happy? And rowdy when I'm scared? I hope you don't really feel as stressed as I do.* Karen closed her eyes and breathed deep, longing to unwind. Eventually, her hands still on her abdomen, she drifted off into sleep.

The next day was a hectic one at work as deadlines loomed regarding the scholastic testing the following week. This latest deadline, in addition to the pressure of trying to solve her scheduling problem, left her with a persistent headache.

She was also nervous about her ultrasound appointment that afternoon. An ultrasound was a standard request by an adoption agency to verify that the baby was healthy. Initially, Karen had been reluctant to have one, fearing she might become even more attached to her child once she saw it. However, lately she had become more resigned to the fact that it was necessary.

By mid-afternoon she had done all that she could that day in preparation for the testing. Sitting at her desk, she once again stared at the large calendar hanging on the wall. *What if I were to reschedule those school visits and move them all into the next couple months?* It was an intriguing concept, one that might possibly work. *But . . .what will I use as my excuse for doing so, when I call to reschedule or when my boss asks about it?* As she straightened the papers on her desk she began to like the idea more and more. After mentally taking inventory of the projects that awaited her the next day, she left for her appointment.

Lying on the table in the darkened room Karen glanced nervously, reluctantly, at the monitor with its shades of black and gray. Beginning to recognize an outline, she looked away quickly. A moment later she found that her eyes had wandered back to the screen, and this time they stayed there.

"I understand you're placing the baby for adoption," the woman asked nervously. "Do you want me to adjust the monitor away from you?"

"No, I'm fine."

"OK. I also usually describe everything that I'm seeing. Do you want me to still do that or not?"

"Sure. Tell me what you see," Karen was unsure of what she really wanted.

"Here's the head," she announced as she moved the instrument around. "Here's the spine, it's normal. And the legs, I see the baby's quite active." She paused, then asked, "Do you want to know the sex of the baby?"

Karen's heart jumped. She believed down deep that it was a girl— she'd seen her in the dream. Yet what if it was a boy? What would that do to the dream and the faith that Karen had attached to it? Her heart raced. Although she wanted to know, she also feared that it might destroy the hope she had been clinging to. "I think it's a girl. Yes, please tell me."

After locating just the right angle, the woman smiled broadly. "You're right. It's a girl."

Elated at the confirmation, Karen beamed. She also realized that her love for the baby was growing as it became more real. *God, I'm going to need You to help me let go when the time comes. I don't know how I'll be able to do it.*

That evening after dinner Emily showed up. "Come on in," Karen beckoned as she held open the door; suddenly realizing that the younger woman had brought her daughter Katie with her. She hadn't seen the baby when she peered through the curtain to see who was knocking.

They sat in the living room and chatted, making plans to eat at their favorite Mexican restaurant during the weekend. Although Karen tried to focus on the conversation, she kept getting distracted by her friend's infant. She deliberately kept her eyes glued on Emily's face, refusing to look away at anything. *I'll pretend that she's not even here,* Karen decided about the child.

"Would you hold her while I use the bathroom?" Emily asked as she passed her daughter to her without waiting for an answer. Caught off guard, Karen had no choice but to hold out her hands and accept the bundle, wrapped in a fuzzy yellow one-piece sleeper. Sitting on the couch with her, Karen looked into her face and was intrigued by her large brown eyes. Remembering her dream, she knew that her daughter would have brown eyes also, just like Rick. Tears welled up momentarily, but Emily striding into the room again and reaching for her daughter interrupted her thoughts.

"Thanks." Emily hoisted the baby onto one hip. "Isn't she just the cutest baby you've ever seen? It's hard to say because all my babies were so adorable, but Grant and I think she may be the cutest yet." Karen was grateful for Emily's loquaciousness because it kept her from having to respond. "Are you hungry, sweetie?" the younger woman cooed to her infant.

Karen felt a pain in her chest at the word "sweetie." How she longed to hold her own baby. *I can't think things like that,* she reminded herself stubbornly.

"What's wrong Karen?" Emily asked gently. "You look horrible."

"Emily, I just can't talk about it," she said firmly, her shaking shoulders contradicting the determination in her voice. "I wish I could." She swallowed. "But thank you for caring. It's not that I don't trust you, it's just that I've made a promise of sorts. . . . There are other people involved in this . . ." Her voice trailed off.

Emily sighed. "Well, do what you have to do. But if you decide you want to talk, I'm here." She walked toward the door. "Grant and I are praying for you," she said over her shoulder as she left.

Once Emily was gone, Karen burst into tears. *All I do is cry lately,* she chided herself. But she felt so hopeless, so alone. *I have no control over anything,* she wailed. *And no one to talk to!*

That evening she found herself in front of the television, flipping aimlessly through channels once again. Scanning the channels, she stumbled upon *A Baby Story* again on TLC. *Apparently it's on every day, featuring a different couple and their delivery.* This time she didn't change the channel immediately although her heart began to beat wildly. She felt pangs of nausea at the thought of eventually going through the same things. However, she focused on the program, making herself watch it. This time she made it almost to the end of the show before panicking and turning it off, emotionally drained. *I can't do it. I just can't do it by myself,* she thought as she cried softly on the couch. *I need someone!*

Once again she poured out her heart to God before climbing into bed. As she lay there, she remembered an interview with G. Gordon Liddy that she had once heard. Although he was a very powerful and strong man now, earlier in life he faced many fears and had learned to deal with them head-on. He discussed how, whenever he was afraid of something, he would make himself experience that thing again and again until he noticed that a confidence would eventually replace the fear.

That might work for me! Perhaps it would be a way of dealing with this. Karen smiled, suddenly not so overwhelmed. Vowing to watch *A Baby Story* every day after work until she was no longer terrified, she placed her hands on her stomach and said aloud to Sweetie, "Well, it won't hurt to give it a try. Somehow, we'll get through this."

WEEK 24

Karen awoke from a fitful sleep to the sound of the phone piercing the darkness. After struggling to locate it on her nightstand, she mumbled, "Hello."

"Hey, how are you?" She recognized Rick's voice and sat up in bed, rubbing her eyes and looking for her alarm clock. Barely 6:00, she noted, wondering what was going on. "I'm going to be in town today and wondered if you wanted to eat dinner together tonight?"

"Uh . . . I don't know," she stuttered, attempting to wake up and gather her wits about her. "I have a trip planned, and I am not sure what time I'll get back." She paused, hoping that he wouldn't push the idea.

"OK. Well I've missed seeing you the last two times that I've been out that way. You haven't been yourself on the phone lately, and I'm worried." He at least sounded sincere.

I must keep my focus, she reminded herself quickly. *I can't afford to let him see me. One look at me, and he will figure everything out.*

Frustration evident in his voice, he said, "I'll call you late this afternoon to see if you're back." He paused momentarily. "Perhaps I should just show up at your door once I see your car is back and whisk you off to dinner."

Her heart pounding ferociously, Karen lay back in bed after the call and wondered whether he would ever really just appear like that. *I can't keep putting him off indefinitely,* she realized. *How can I ever manage to keep this secret from him? It's challenging enough doing it with everyone else.* Rolling over, she glanced at the window. Sunlight was peeping between the slats of the blinds. Her mind wandered. *I thought this would be easier, since he lives several hours away, but it seems as if lately he's been around quite frequently.*

Whatever possessed me to lie to Rick and tell him that I had an abortion? It had been almost 10 weeks ago, yet she cringed as her mind returned to the phone calls leading up to her lie, reliving the intense pain in his voice during each conversation. The pressure had been too much to handle.

I know that the lie was wrong. She had regretted it immediately, and had wished many times that she hadn't chosen that route. Yet she had.

Her alarm clock sounded, jarring her from her thoughts. *OK, time to switch into my work mood and pretend that everything is fine,* she thought on her way to the shower. She prayed her constant morning prayer: *God, please give me strength for today.*

Standing in front of her full-length mirror after dressing, Karen turned from side to side as she scrutinized her navy dress pants and loose fitting sweater. *So far, so good,* she thought to herself. For the first time in her life she was grateful for being a little overweight, since the way that she was built helped camouflage her growing midriff.

Karen found it difficult to concentrate on her work throughout the morning. Her heart began to race each time she thought of him showing up unannounced. She welcomed the trip that she had scheduled for that afternoon, for it offered a change of scenery and uninterrupted time to think. Plus, it would get her out of the office, in case he happened to turn up.

Gathering a few remaining papers from her desk, she placed them in her leather briefcase. After grabbing a quick lunch in the cafeteria, she pulled out of the parking lot by 12:30, exactly on time.

Snow fell lightly from the overcast gray sky, and the roads were wet, but there was no accumulation.Karen fidgeted with the CD player, trying several artists, quickly popping the disk out and searching for another one that would calm her nerves. *Nothing seems to do the trick today,* she thought in frustration. *Why not?* Restless, worried, and anxious, she had become weary of the constant charade.

Two hours later she arrived at the elementary school where she was to make her presentation. As if in a daze, she set up her PowerPoint and gave her talk with robotic precision. The students responded positively to her 40-minute program, and the teaching staff expressed their appreciation of her visit.

On her trip home, Karen again struggled with exhaustion. Her mind quickly returned to Rick. *What will I do if he really stops by? I have nowhere to turn, no escape.* She understood that eventually he would find out that she had deceived him, that she was still pregnant. But she didn't want it to be today!

Karen gritted her teeth as she drove. As hard as she tried to put strategies into place that would keep her two worlds separate, she felt emotionally and physically exhausted by the end of each day.

The sun was just beginning to set as she arrived home. After pulling into her regular parking space out of habit, she quickly moved her car to a nearby parking area, attempting to hide it from Rick, should he drive by looking for her.

Once inside her warm apartment, she was relieved to find a message on her answering machine letting her know that he was running behind schedule and wouldn't have time for dinner. He closed by saying that he would call her in a day or two. *Phew!* Relief surged through her body. *At least I don't have to worry about that tonight.*

Needing a diversion, something to take her mind away from the stresses that consumed her more each day, she sat in the living room with all of the lights out and just one candle burning. Since her car wasn't parked out front and no lights were on, she felt confident that her neighbors would think that she was gone, and thus no one would disturb her.

Sinking into the green chair, she felt soothed by the CD softly playing in the background. She closed her eyes and pictured one of the happier times that she and Rick had spent together. They had driven to the nearby mountains on a sunny fall day and had a picnic that he had carefully prepared. After a relaxing meal and resting and talking for an hour, they drove a few miles farther and wandered through a local fruit stand. It was grape harvest time in New England, and they found lattice-crust grape pies in large tin pie plates, purple jams and jellies in small glass jars with swatches of colorful material draped on the top and tied with red ribbons, and a multitude of white, purple, and dark-blue grapes in quart baskets. The rich aroma of grapes hung in the air throughout the market and halfway into the street. She could still smell them in her mind.

Karen basked in that memory. Yes, she and Rick had shared some wonderful times. They had laughed frequently, more than she could ever remember laughing before. And he had comforted her through her divorce and supported her throughout her career transition. *Why can't he comfort and support me now?* Her heart ached. She longed to return to those joyous times again, to erase the pain of the past few months.

Tears streamed down her cheeks as she slowly eased out of those memories and back to harsh reality. Sitting alone in her apartment, she couldn't remember a time when she had felt so alone. *Father, please help me,* she prayed. But the emotional burden wouldn't budge.

For days she had begun to feel that her prayers were not reaching farther than the ceiling. *Where are You, God?* she questioned more and more often. *I believe that You're there, yet I can't feel You. I'm so restless and so alone.*

Dear God, please hold me and comfort me. Please let me know that You're near.

Soft music continued to play as she sat, her eyes closed. Although she wasn't sure exactly when the pressure began to lift, within a few minutes she felt noticeably better. *Thank You for showing me You're still there.*

After listening to the CD for a little while longer, Karen felt convicted to call Sandy and make things right with her. She had always felt guilty for letting her friend believe a lie about the abortion.

Her heart raced as she dialed Sandy's number and each second seemed like an eternity. "Hello."

"Hi, Sandy," Karen's voice shook. "What are you up to tonight?"

"Not much. Are you OK?" she asked, perplexed at the sound of Karen's voice. "You sound tired or something."

"I'm fine." Karen tried to sound convincing.

They chatted for a while about their day and other odds and ends. Eventually Karen knew that she couldn't put off her confession any longer and soon the truth was spilling out. "Sandy, I have a confession to make."

"Oh?"

She plunged ahead lest she lose her nerve. "I never had an abortion, Sandy. I only told Rick that I did so he'd leave me alone."

The woman gasped. "What are you saying?" A long pause. "Are you still pregnant?" Karen could hear excitement in her voice.

"Yes," Karen admitted. The relief felt good.

"I'm so glad! I've felt very guilty for encouraging you to have an abortion."

"You didn't encourage me. I just asked your opinion, and you gave it to me, that's all. Sandy, will you forgive me for lying to you?"

"Of course!" her friend exclaimed. "I know how Rick can be. He has a knack for making people feel bad for him and getting them to do things that he wants."

"Yeah, that's him," Karen agreed. "I just couldn't stand to hear him in such pain every night on the phone."

"You know, Rick called me many times early on, so upset about the pregnancy, and feeling terrible, because he didn't know what to do for you."

"I get so angry at him sometimes, feeling very alone and abandoned."

"I'm sure you do!" Sandy said. "I don't think I would have handled this whole situation like you have. I would have been very hard on him."

The two talked for more than an hour. Karen shared with Sandy the promise that God had made to her, and explained how He had led her thus far. "He's shown me what clothes to wear, what adoption agency to choose, and even what to ask for as far as adoptive parents are concerned."

"Wow! What an awesome miracle."

"Yes, but I still get nervous about the future—about the unknown. Yet I have a peace that I'll get through it somehow—because of the promise." Hearing herself say it out loud made Karen believe it even more.

"So what are you going to do about your job?" Sandy asked curiously. "I take it that's why you've been searching for other employment?"

"Yes. I was very frustrated when nothing opened up, since I've always been able to get jobs easily. I don't know, though. I'm thinking now that maybe God has another plan. That I need to be patient and have faith until I see what that is."

"That must be hard."

"Yeah, but there's nothing I can do about it." Karen chuckled. "One day at a time."

At the end of the conversation Sandy reminded her, "You know, you really have to tell Rick."

"I know. You're right." Karen sighed.

"He's a big boy, and he'll learn to deal with it. You've given him a 10-week break, which is much more than I would have done."

WEEK 25

The sun glistened off patches of snow in the yard, glinting through the picture window into Karen's apartment. Winter wasn't totally over, but spring was on its way.

Her mind wandered that Sunday afternoon as she lay on the couch. After her conversation with Sandy a few days before her thoughts had been consumed with whether or not she should confess to Rick that she was still pregnant. Some moments she wanted to blurt it all out. Her life was difficult enough without this added stress. However, she wasn't sure what his reaction would be. *Am I afraid that I'll completely lose him? Hasn't that happened already?* She felt disgusted with herself for still wanting to cling to Rick, despite her anger at him.

Suddenly her finger froze on the television remote, her attention caught by an interview of Faith Hill, a beautiful country music singer. She was a favorite of Karen's, and at first just the music kept her attention. Then, just before a commercial, a short teaser for an upcoming segment showed her talking about being adopted.

As the show continued Karen listened to Faith openly discuss her experience. The interviewer spoke with her siblings, who had welcomed her into the family as one of their own. Her adoptive parents had encouraged and nurtured her musical talents. In the final segment Faith described meeting her birth mother.

By now Karen sat cross-legged on the couch. The music aspect of Faith's story especially intrigued her as she wondered what biological influences had produced such a strong voice and great musical talent. *I wonder who her real father is?*

The program interspersed Faith's songs between the interview segments. Karen noticed that during the musical portions her baby was active, moving and kicking frequently. Ever since the concert that she and Sandy had attended she had paid close attention to the child's response to music. She'd also grown more convinced that Sweetie should be with a family who was involved in music, and who would nurture and encourage any talent the child might have.

At the end of the program Karen clicked off the television and nestled down on the couch for a nap. Yet her mind wouldn't shut off. The interview had encouraged her, given her hope—yes, perhaps a sort of confirmation of her choice to place her baby for adoption.

I have so much that I'd like to share with Rick . . . that is, if I tell him the truth, and once he gets over the initial shock again. The memory of his fear made her cringe. She longed to reassure him that somehow everything would turn out all right. *He's missed 10 weeks of decisions, of miracles, and of the special assurance that God has provided me.* While she had become increasingly more comfortable with God's promise to her, she couldn't expect Rick to understand or to be anything but terrified.

How can I expect him to understand where I'm at right now in my thought process? How can I . . . She finally drifted off to sleep.

Startled, Karen awakened to the phone ringing. She fumbled to locate the portable. "Hello," she said, half asleep.

"Hello," came a deep voice on the other end of the line.

"How are you?" she asked, wondering if this was still part of her dream.

"I'm fine. How are you?" Rick asked, sounding concerned.

"I've been better," she replied truthfully.

"I'm sure it's hard. It'll take time to heal."

You're sure it's hard? His response angered her. He sounded as if the whole thing was no big deal now. As long as the problem had gone away, he was unconcerned. Trying to refocus, she said, "There's something that I want to talk with you about, but I just can't find the words."

"Just open your mouth and spit it out."

"It's not that easy." Karen sighed heavily. "Listen, I'm going to hang up and call you back in a few minutes, when I get my thoughts together." She needed to wake up. "When I phone, I don't want you to say a word, just let me speak until I get this out. OK?"

"All right." Rick sounded hesitant, worried.

For almost 20 minutes she paced the living room, praying for courage and the right words. *This is so hard! Why can't I just say it?* Her mind flashed back to the first time that she had told him she was pregnant. She could still hear the pain in his voice, and it sent chills up her spine. *Can I go through this again?*

Picking up the phone, her hand shook as she dialed the number. She wanted to hang up, but refused to let herself press the off button. *Just do it.*

"Hello." This time he sounded nervous.

Taking a deep breath, she charged ahead. "Rick, I wasn't honest with you when I told you that I had had an abortion. You were putting so much pressure on me that I didn't know what else to do." Catching another breath, she pressed on. "I thought that if I told you I had an abortion you'd leave me alone and have your care-free life back again." *There. I did it.*

Absolutely no response. Her heart pounded. The silence was worse than anything he could say or do. *Say something! Anything!* she screamed in her mind. Finally she couldn't stand it any longer and asked, "Do you want to hang up now?"

A very subdued voice answered, "No, that wouldn't be the responsible thing to do."

Responsible! Karen wanted to scream. She didn't want responsibility—she needed compassion, love, and caring. Working to control her growing anger, she continued, "I'm sorry, Rick. I thought it was the right thing to do at the time. You were upset and kept pressuring me. I couldn't bear to hear your pain each night on the phone when I could barely handle my own."

His voice was so weak she could hardly make out what he was saying. "How far along are you?"

"Almost six months. But no one knows. Thanks to my 'camouflage clothing' I look pretty normal."

"You're at the school everyday, and no one has noticed? How can that be?" he asked in disbelief.

"Well, I have the advantage of having the right kind of body to hide this."

"I saw you at the funeral a while ago, and you looked great. I just can't believe this!"

"Yes, and you couldn't tell that I was pregnant, could you? See what I'm talking about?"

"What are your plans? You can't expect to get to nine months pregnant and still have no one notice!"

"I've decided on adoption. I think it's best for all of us. I've done some research and have found a licensed agency, and they've sent me the paperwork." After a pause, she added, "I'm hoping to find the courage to fill them out one of these days."

"And what about your job? How long do you plan to stay there?" he inquired nervously.

"I'm working on getting a leave-of-absence for the last month or two."

Rick inhaled deeply, then slowly let it out, sighing audibly, "I feel worse than the first time you told me."

"I thought seriously about never telling you—just going through with it by myself. But keeping this from you was getting harder and harder. I also need you to help me with the adoption paperwork."

Although sounding defeated and tired, he muttered, "You could have kept it from me. I wouldn't have minded."

"Well, I gave you 10 weeks of ignorant bliss!" Her anger boiled from deep within. How dare he? Did he have any idea what she was going through? How could he abandon her like this? *I thought you loved me,* she wanted to shout. *Yet you won't even be supportive!*

"Ignorant bliss is good." His words were completely devoid of emotion.

Throwing the phone against the wall, she burst into tears. She was angry that he was so selfish. Angry that he didn't love her more than he did. And angry that she had let herself fall for someone like him. *What was I thinking?*

Somehow she forced herself to calm down before walking over to where the phone lay. Out of habit she placed the receiver to her ear. No dial tone. *What does that mean?* "Hello?"

She heard his voice on the other end. "I'm still here."

"Why do you have to frustrate me so!"

"I'm sorry. You caught me off-guard tonight, and it's going to take a while for this to sink in again."

Sitting on the floor, her back braced against the wall, she managed to reply, "Rick, I want to share something with you. Perhaps it'll give you peace, as it did me. After you and I tried to figure out a solution to this problem, I got on my knees one night and asked God for an answer. I refused to get up until He showed me what to do. He made me a promise that night, Rick. He assured me that if I didn't have an abortion, that He would 'close their eyes.' He's going to work this out."

"I don't know what to say." She couldn't decide whether he was being sincere or flippant.

"I know it's a lot to comprehend. I'm the one that heard the promise, not you, so I don't expect you to understand." Getting up from the floor, she went to the couch. "I've experienced many miracles. Times where God has comforted me and kept others from noticing my pregnancy."

"I want to believe that everything will turn out fine," he said despondently.

"About the adoption—I need you to complete some paperwork," she said hesitantly. *How can I expect him to fill out his part when I can't bring myself to do mine?*

Fear echoed in his deep voice. "I'll give you whatever information you need, but I don't want my name on anything."

"I won't put your name on the birth certificate," she assured him. She had already come to the same conclusion. "However, the adoption papers are strictly confidential, and you don't have to worry about providing your information."

"Don't be so sure." *He can be so paranoid.*

"I've learned a lot about this process during the past few months. In order for us to find the best parents, we have to do the paperwork completely." Her heart raced. What if he doesn't help with this? *What if we don't find parents?* "Adoptive parents are very leery when a father doesn't cooperate, because it takes longer to finalize the adoption."

"Let me think about it, and I'll get back to you."

"OK. Will you call tomorrow night?" Although she felt frustrated, she knew it would be of no use to push him. He would just become more stubborn and reluctant to cooperate.

"Yes." That was all he said before hanging up.

That evening, lying in bed with her hands on her stomach, Karen's mind kept returning to the interview that she had seen. *Faith Hill seems to be well-adjusted and happy,* she reassured herself. *And her adoptive parents love her so much. Adoption is the best thing for Sweetie, I know it is. It's just so hard. Will I be able to go through with it? What if . . .*

Her mind jumped back to a phone conversation that she had had with Kathleen from the adoption agency. The woman had shared samples of thank-you letters that adoptive parents had written to the birth mothers, expressing their love and joy for the children that had blessed their lives. A peace warmed Karen's heart as she drifted off to sleep, once again lost in vivid dreams.

She could not take her eyes off the teenager. About 16 years old, the dark-haired young woman stood before a large audience, singing in a strong voice, eyes closed, one hand reaching skyward. Part of an outdoor youth rally, the stage was large and crowded with a full band and grand piano. When the praise-and-worship song ended, the teenager took a bow. Flipping her head back, her hair glistened in the sun. She glanced to the side of the stage, where Karen stood, as if searching for someone. The girl's brown eyes, framed by long dark lashes, locked with Karen's. Instantly Karen recognized those eyes.

WEEK 28

Slipping the video into the VCR, Karen walked slowly toward the couch, weary after a long day at work. During the past six weeks she had traveled extensively for her job, and although it had accomplished her goal of completing her spring trips early, it had been exhausting. Sitting down, she pulled her legs up against her and tried to get comfortable. Her stomach was getting large, and comfortable had become a relative term.

As the video began, she smiled at the thought of relaxing to 30 minutes of music by her favorite southern gospel group. The first song was upbeat and catchy. Until she had met Rick, she'd never listened to southern gospel music. Now she had grown to enjoy it because of the countless hours they spent listening to it together.

The second song prompted memories of the time when she and Rick had attended that outdoor southern gospel festival in the foothills of Pennsylvania. Up until that night—that fateful night—they had been blissfully happy together. *I wish we could have just stayed like that forever,* she thought wistfully.

The baby's strong kicking drew her thoughts back to the living room. The video was still playing, a song just ending. In the stillness of her apartment, blinds drawn tightly, Karen placed her hands on her abdomen. *Hey, you're sure enjoying the music, aren't you?* She smiled. *You're going to be musical, that's for sure.* Excitement surged through her. *I'm getting attached to you, Sweetie. I love you.* But then sadness replaced the excitement. *And I'm never going to get to know you.* She could feel the tears starting. *Don't cry. Don't.*

Miraculously, she managed to hold the tears back. Yawning as the tape ended, she headed to bed, a bittersweet feeling enveloping her as memories of happier times still lingered in her mind. *I'll just get on with my life,* she tried to convince herself. *It'll be fine. This is the best way.*

As she walked down the hallway at school the next morning, she realized what a toll the uncertainty about her future was taking. It was getting harder and harder to go to work, to put on a smile, and to be constantly on guard. While she loved her job and enjoyed the students and her coworkers, the constant fear was always present.

Grabbing the yellow piece of paper taped to her office door, she struggled to open it with one hand while unlocking the door with the other. She dropped her purse into her chair and hung her coat on the nearby coat stand. Reading the note a second time she mumbled nervously, "I wonder what my boss wants with me this early in the day?"

After stalling for a few more minutes, she made her way cautiously down to the principal's office, notebook strategically placed in front of her stomach. Smiling, she tried to be as upbeat as possible. "How's your morning going so far?" she inquired, wondering about what the principal wanted.

"Oh, hello Karen," he began as he pulled some papers together on his desk. "Sit down."

"What's up?" she asked nervously, imagining the worst. *I'm just paranoid,* she reminded herself. *He doesn't know what's going on. Just stay calm and everything will be all right.*

"I have a small job for you," he began matter-of-factly. "I just found out that the registrar will be gone for six weeks this summer, and I need someone to send out transcripts and make sure those types of things get done in his absence."

Relieved that he hadn't discovered her secret, she sighed. She was always worried that someone would notice her growing stomach. Although it wasn't bad news that he had given her, it still presented a problem in light of her plans for a leave of absence.

Before she could respond, the phone beeped, and Mr. Harrington excused himself. Thankful for a moment to gather her thoughts, her mind churned. *I haven't even asked for the leave yet, so what should I say to this request?* Her heart beat faster. *God, give me the words to say!*

A moment later the principal hung up and turned to face her again. "I apologize—that was a call I'd been waiting for."

"No problem," she assured him, still stalling for time.

"I don't think these added responsibilities will take much of your time. Just open the mail each day and get the transcript requests sent out promptly."

"I'm sure I can help." Why had she said that for? Now she had gotten herself into a jam. She couldn't very well be mailing transcripts from her hideaway, wherever that might be. She sighed. *Oh well. Get back to work and worry about it later.*

The rest of the morning was uneventful. Karen finished a project for scholastic testing and then reviewed her schedule for the remainder of the school year. Sitting in her comfortable chair, she rolled back and swung around to gaze at the large blue and white calendar hanging on the wall behind her. Smiling she thought, *Since moving those school visits earlier, I've already finished most of them, and within the next couple of weeks I'll have the rest complete.*

The calendar had many other events written across it, each notation indicating a program on campus which she was expected to attend, yet wasn't responsible for. *My calendar looks full, so there's nothing to tip anyone off to my impending leave at this point. Things that I'm in charge of are covered, which is what matters.*

Jenni ambled into Karen's office, interrupting her thoughts. "Hi, what's going on with you today?" the girl asked as she slipped into a chair and set her book bag down.

"Hi, Jenni. How's school going?" Karen rolled her chair back behind her desk, hiding her stomach.

"School's fine. Hey, and I'm getting along better with my parents these days."

"Good!"

"The other night I asked my mom what she would think about me looking for my birth-mother, and she was actually cool with the idea," Jenni beamed.

Karen gulped. "When are you going to begin looking?"

"Probably this summer." She paused briefly, "I'm a little nervous. I want to meet her . . . but I'm scared."

"What makes you nervous?"

"I don't know. Not sure what to expect, I guess. What if she's some wacko or something?" The girl smiled sheepishly. "Or what if she doesn't *want* to meet me? I mean, she didn't want me in the first place."

The words cut like a knife, and Karen worked to maintain composure. "Do you think that not knowing what she's like might be safer than taking the risk of finding out?"

"Yeah, maybe. It's so confusing."

"You know, just because she gave you up doesn't necessarily mean she didn't want you. You don't know her circumstances . . ." Her voice trailed off. What would she tell Sweetie, years from now, if she ever saw her again?

"But I can't imagine giving your baby away if you loved it." Sadness tinged Jenni's voice. "How could anyone do that? I suppose she thought I would mess up her life." The girl tried to smile but failed.

"No, Jenni," Karen insisted softly. *What should I say?* she wondered. "Maybe she wasn't in a position where she could have given you the care you deserved."

The girl shrugged. "Maybe. At any rate, I think I want to meet her. I'll ask her why, if I'm brave enough."

The bell rang. "Pray about it, Jenni. If it's meant to be, then God will work it out."

"Thanks," the girl said over her shoulder as she departed for class.

After Jenni left Karen sat at her desk and twirled a pencil. How would Sweetie react when she found out she was adopted? What kind of person would she think her birth mother was? Would she feel unwanted? *But I love you,* Karen wanted to scream. *I love you. I don't want to give you up! God, let her understand,* she prayed silently. *Let her know it wasn't a lack of love.*

That evening, back in her apartment, Karen changed into a large burgundy sweatshirt and maternity jeans. *What do I want for supper?* she wondered as she opened the refrigerator door. Nothing looked appealing. However, the thought of pizza, loaded with every vegetable imaginable, made her mouth water. Reaching for the phone, she dialed the number she had memorized months earlier. Pizza was what she craved the most.

After watching the news and finishing supper, Karen reached for the phone to call Sandy.

"Hello."

"Hi, Sandy. Any excitement down there?"

"Hey, I was going to call you later."

"Oh?"

"Just wanted to check on you and see how you're doing."

"I don't know what I'd do without you! I could never make it through this, that's for sure." Karen was more grateful every day that she had told her friend the truth.

"How's Sarah doing?"

"Fine. She e-mails several times a week. Her classes are going well, and she's still seeing that guy she met."

"I'm glad she's doing well. I'm sure that's a relief—one less thing you have to worry about right now."

"True. I couldn't handle one more challenge."

"Have you spoken to Rick lately?" Sandy asked hesitantly.

"No." Sadness filled Karen's voice. "We've not spoken since the night I called him to tell him I was still pregnant."

"I figured as much. He and I have spoken a couple of times since then, but each time I ask about you, he gets quiet and changes the subject."

Tears welled in Karen's eyes, but she refused to give in. *I loved him, but . . .*

Sandy changed the subject. "How's the adoption process going?"

"OK, I guess. Kathleen has called several times to check on me. Lately she keeps asking when I'm going to mail the paperwork back. I know I should send it soon."

"Have you made plans to attend a Lamaze class?"

"No, you need a coach for Lamaze, and I don't have one," Karen snapped with resentment. "Besides, that's why I've been watching TLC. I've been using that as a refresher course."

"Have you asked Rick to be your coach?"

"Come on!" Karen said sarcastically. "He hasn't called since I told him the truth, so I guess that's sort of a hint that I'm on my own."

"How about if I were to coach you? I'd be available by summer—after all, I'm a teacher and have the summer off. I could come up and spend a week or two."

"That's a thought," Karen said slowly. "But I've been working on plans for a leave of absence and will most likely be in Nashville by then."

"Nashville? Why Nashville? Do you know someone there?"

"No, just the opposite. I don't know anyone there." Karen sighed heavily. "I want to be anonymous . . . to have no pressure to hide . . . no fear of being discovered . . . to be able to walk in the mall, go to a restaurant, and not worry anymore."

"I can only imagine."

"I also chose Nashville because of the music scene. It's been so long since I've done any songwriting and going there might inspire my creativity again." Karen felt excited at the thought—something to alleviate the sadness of saying goodbye to Sweetie.

"How long will you stay?"

"Right now I'm leaning toward two months. I wish I could pick up and go now, but I know I would attract unwanted attention if I were to request that much time off. I still have three months to go."

"How will you support yourself while you're there?"

"Well, I mentioned my idea to Kathleen, and she told me that the adoptive family would cover all of my living expenses, so money's no problem."

"Great!"

"Yeah, now I just have to get my nerve up to request the time off. Everyone is already so overworked at the school that I feel extremely guilty asking for a two-month leave. I think I might ask for two to three weeks off initially, and then find a reason to extend it as I go along. I'm so afraid that if I go for two months off all at once they'll just say no."

"Keep praying about it. God will work things out."

"I know."

After a moment Sandy asked, "How about if I meet you in Nashville and be your coach?"

Karen smiled to herself. "Would you really do that for me?"

"Of course!"

That night Karen lay in bed with her hands on her stomach, thinking about her future. *Things are coming together, slowly but surely.* She again smiled as she thought about all of the little ways in which God was leading, guiding her through this maze in which she couldn't see the end. *Every day that I go to work and have a productive day is a good one.* Her career was extremely important to her. *It's all I have left,* she realized despairingly. *I can't lose that too.*

I only have to make it through these next four weeks, and then it'll be downhill from there once I get to Nashville. It was the thought that kept her going.

Then her mind went back to the divine promise. She remembered it as vividly as if it had happened just last night. *"I can shut their eyes."* That was pretty bold assurance, she told herself. *Apparently God will keep people from noticing that I'm pregnant until I get to Nashville . . . and then once I'm there, it won't matter anymore! Maybe this really can work out. Maybe I can make it through with no one finding out.*

WEEK 29

Karen hurried through the door of her apartment, quickly locking it behind her. Doubling over in agony, she moaned, holding her midsection with both hands. She could barely breathe as the pain pierced her like a knife. *Oh . . . this hurts!* Again she moaned, still gripping her stomach.

What's wrong? she wondered as the wave of pain finally subsided and she could once again stand up straight. After removing her spring dress coat, she walked to the living room and sank onto the green and burgundy couch, leaning back on one of the large cushions and closing her eyes.

She had spent the past three hours in her office trying to complete an important project, the abdominal pain sweeping through her every 40 minutes. Finally at noon she had given up, telling the secretary that she was ill and was going home for the day.

Propping her feet up on a pillow, Karen lay on the couch, stomach protruding noticeably. *Maybe if I can relax these pains will go away,* she tried to reassure herself. Closing her eyes, she deliberately breathed deeply. Just as she was starting to relax, another wave of pain engulfed her. Sitting upright, she worked to breathe through the episode.

By 3:00 she had reached a state of panic. Steady and regular, the pains had not subsided as she had hoped. Fearful, she telephoned her physician.

"Dr. Jacobson's office. May I help you?"

"This is Karen Williams. I've been having pains—kind of like contractions—all day long, and I need to know what to do to make them stop."

"Hold on, let me get the nurse."

A few moments later the receptionist came back on the line. "Karen, the nurse said that you need to be seen. Can you come in right away?"

Startled, she drew a deep breath and replied, "Sure, I'll be there in 20 minutes."

As she drove along the winding back roads to town everything seemed to be in slow motion. A red car, barely moving, passed by in the opposite lane. Black and white cows in a nearby field stood still, as if they were part of a painting. The stoplight at the intersection in town was stuck on red.

The song on the radio faded in and out as Karen's mind sorted through thoughts word by word, even letter by letter.

Once at the office, she let the nurse escort her down the hall and into a room. Soon Dr. Jacobson rushed in. "What's going on?" he inquired, taking a seat in a chair across from hers. Karen felt comfortable with him. He always dealt with her in a caring and compassionate way.

"I've been having pains on and off all day. What can I do to make them stop?"

"What do you mean by 'having pains all day'? Be more specific."

"Well, I began noticing them around 9:00 this morning. Every so often they would happen, and eventually I started timing them. They've been coming every 40 minutes."

"When was the last one?"

"Right before I left for your office."

"I don't like the sound of that. Braxton-Hicks contractions are occasional and sporadic, not regular." He glanced inside her chart and continued, "You're not far enough along to be having false labor." Standing up he added, "The nurse will be back in and give you something to change into. I want to check you, to make sure there's nothing to worry about, and then we can start you on some medication to stop the pain and prevent further episodes."

After the exam Dr. Jacobson told her, "You aren't dilating yet, which is what I wanted to make sure of." He wrote on his prescription pad and then tore off the sheet. "Start taking this tonight. Additionally, you need to have as much bed rest as possible. Lay on your left side, totally flat, or even put a pillow under your hips, and stay there until you are feeling better and aren't having anymore pain."

Stunned, she protested, "Well, I have to go to work tomorrow."

"Not if you aren't feeling better!" he ordered, looking at her with one eyebrow raised. "You've got to take care of yourself and this baby."

After filling the prescription and picking up a sandwich at a Subway, Karen drove home and locked herself in her apartment. She spent the remainder of the evening lying on her left side, watching television. *What am I going to do,* she wondered, discouraged. *I have to go to work tomorrow!*

By bedtime she was relieved to realize that she hadn't had any contractions for several hours. Crawling in between the sheets she snuggled down on her left side again, exhausted from the emotional and physical stress of the day. However, her mind wouldn't let her rest.

I really need to send in the adoption paperwork tomorrow morning, she told herself. *The forms have been complete for several weeks—I don't know why I keep stalling. But after what happened today I can't play around anymore.* Her mind ran wild. *What if I waited until the very end to send in the papers, and Sweetie was born before the agency could find adoptive parents? I just couldn't leave her alone in a hospital . . . without parents to take her home and love her.* All of a sudden her thoughts were back to where they had wandered so many times before. *I would keep her. I'd find a way to do it somehow. I'd . . .* Eventually she drifted off into a troubled sleep.

First thing the next morning Karen took the manila envelope down to the post office. As she stood in line, her eyes moist and her heart heavy, she glanced down at the package in her hands. Finally, when it was her turn at the counter, all she could manage to say was, "Overnight, please." That was done, at last. "There, I did it," she said out loud in her car. "It's out of my hands."

During the next couple days she took her medication faithfully and made a conscious effort to relax. At her doctor's advice she had worked shorter days and had come home each afternoon, resting as much as possible, and was feeling significantly better.

However, by the end of the week she began to experience regular contractions again. The first one hit mid-morning, soon after she had left a staff meeting. Going home early, she telephoned the doctor's office and once again the receptionist told her to come in.

"Karen," the doctor began. "I'm going to give you an injection and place you on a stronger medication." He had a worried expression as he added, "But you need to understand that this is serious. Should you continue to have steady contractions, you'll be forced into complete bed rest, and if they still persist, you'll end up in the hospital."

Stunned, she stared into his eyes, longing for him to smile and explain that it really wasn't that bad. Yet those words never came. "I suspect that these contractions are brought on by stress, Karen. You must relax."

When Sandy called that evening, Karen was still extremely upset.

"Hi, Karen, how was your day?"

"Terrible," she began, sniffling as she explained. "I've had more contractions, and the doctor says it's serious."

"Oh no! What are they going to do?"

"I'm on a new medication. Hopefully it'll work. If it doesn't, he's threatening bed rest. I can't do that . . ." Karen felt herself beginning to panic. It was hard to breathe.

"I know. Stay calm. Remember that everything has worked out so far."

"Yeah, I know." *You've gotten me this far, God. Don't leave me now!*

"Is there anything I can do?"

"Just pray. I mailed off the paperwork to Kathleen this week, and I'm hoping that they find parents soon." Karen tasted the sadness in her own words. It meant that Sweetie would be irreversibly gone.

"I'm sure that was difficult." Sandy stalled, unsure of what to say.

"On days like this I just keep reminding myself of the promise." Karen knew she was reassuring herself as much as she was her friend. "Somehow, down deep, I know that everything will be all right." *Will it?*

"Yes, it will," Sandy reassured.

Two days later Karen returned to the doctor's office for her scheduled recheck to make sure that the new medication was working effectively. "Tell me," he began as he looked at her chart, "have you had any further contractions?"

"No, not really." Karen wasn't really sure. Nothing serious, but . . .

"That doesn't sound convincing. Let me rephrase that question: Have you had *any* pains since you were in two days ago? Even if there were one or two, I need to know about them," the doctor stressed.

"Well, I've had an occasional one, maybe five or six during the past two days, but nothing regular." *Oh, no! What is going to happen now?*

After a few moments of silence, Dr. Jacobson announced, "Karen, I want to refer you to an OB/GYN specialist in the city. There are two reasons for this. First, they are more up to date about what medications to keep you on so that you don't have any further episodes. And second, if you should go into premature labor, they are on staff at the larger hospitals that would be best suited to care for you and the baby."

Stunned, she pleaded, "But I'm doing much better. I don't want another doctor. Nothing bad is going to happen." *I can't do that! I can't leave! I've made other plans!*

"I'm doing this only as a precaution. Let me refer you to Dr. Stephanie Alexander. I hear great things about her." He patted her shoulder. "I just want to make sure all bases are covered."

"What about my plans to go to Nashville for the delivery? Do you think I should push that trip up a bit and go sooner?" Her mind was awhirl. What was happening? She'd had everything so carefully planned out.

With a grim expression he replied, "Unless you go for several weeks with absolutely no pains or contractions, you won't be able to travel anywhere."

Overwhelmed, tears welled in her eyes. "But I have to get to Nashville. I can't stay here once I'm showing." She began to perspire.

"I'll be right back." Excusing himself, he left her alone in the small sterile room. She fought back the tears.

Within minutes he returned, a small piece of paper in hand. "I've made you an appointment to see Dr. Alexander two weeks from Friday. Now don't worry," he comforted, taking Karen's hand. "This is just a precaution. You're going to be fine, and hopefully within a day or two you won't be having anymore contractions."

All the way home she replayed the doctor's words in her mind. "This is just a precaution. You're going to be fine." However, his ultimatum about not traveling to Nashville overrode any reassuring thoughts she could muster.

What will I do if I can't get to Nashville? Karen asked herself again and again. I have all these plans. Once again her mind swept back to the promise. *"I can shut their eyes."* Yes, God made that promise to me, so now I must have faith that I'll be in Nashville within a few weeks. Keep trusting, Karen. It'll be fine.

WEEK 30

Elated and relieved, Karen had gone a full week without further contractions, and life had returned to a normal routine of work and rest. Now she was trying to keep occupied and wait patiently during the next three weeks until she could get the go-ahead from her doctor to make the trip to Nashville. *God, You are in control,* she sang. *Everything is working out.*

Early one morning she awoke before her alarm, inspired to begin working out the details for her time in Nashville. Birds chirped outside the window, and the sun peaked through the mini blinds in her bedroom. Cozy and warm, Karen snuggled beneath the fluffy down comforter, her hands on her stomach as Sweetie moved and kicked rambunctiously. "Apparently, your day begins way before mine does!" she spoke aloud to her daughter.

Thoughts about her leave of absence flooded her mind. She looked forward to her trip with the same excitement as a child anticipates Christmas. Smiling peacefully, she pictured a small apartment—modern, cozy, and with many windows. The weather would be perfect there, plenty of sunshine and no snow or rain. No longer filled with fear and anxiety, her days would be stress-free and relaxing. She could wear comfortable clothes and not worry about hiding her pregnancy.

Music was also a big part of the picture. Envisioning many hours in her apartment with a keyboard, Karen hoped that creativity would return. Music! It soothed and inspired her, bringing out aspects of her personality that otherwise never appeared. She hoped to write new songs, to tap into her creativity that had been buried during the past few months. Would she be able to write about Sweetie? Her heart ached. No, probably not. Not yet, anyway.

Thoughts about labor and delivery also filled her mind. She hoped that she would like her new doctor in Nashville. She'd been fortunate to find Dr. Jacobson and needed to feel comfortable with her new health-care provider. She was also glad that Sandy would be with her at the end to coach her through the physical—and emotional—pain. *I won't be alone,* she reminded herself. More than anything else, it was the loneliness that she couldn't take.

Eventually Karen eased out of her daydream, shut off her alarm before it could ring, and shuffled to the shower. Pulling her robe around her as she walked, she struggled not to waddle. Suddenly, within the past week, she seemed to have blossomed. She was now in a race against time—a contest to see if she could get out of town before her growing girth gave away her secret.

Karen watched her clock with anticipation as she sat in her office that morning. Finally, as soon as businesses were open, Karen shut her office door and telephoned a realtor in Nashville, eager to locate an apartment for the two months she would spend there.

"Century 21, this is Ginny," came a woman's voice with a strong southern accent.

"Hello, I'd like to rent a studio apartment in the Nashville area," Karen began excitedly.

"How long do you need an apartment for?"

"Two months."

"What neighborhood would you like to live in?"

"How about Green Hills?" Karen responded playfully, knowing that it was the most expensive neighborhood in the metropolitan area. "Actually, I'm looking for something in an average area."

"I take it you'll need a furnished place, since it's a short-term lease?"

"Yes."

After a brief pause, during which Karen could hear Ginny typing on her computer, the woman said, "There are several to chose from. How about if I fax you information about each, and you can call me back when you decide which one is right for you?"

Excitedly, Karen thanked her and assured her that she would make a decision within the next 24 hours.

A wave of relief filled her. *It's really happening! It's finally coming together,* she thought to herself as she leaned back in her office chair and smiled. *Everything is going according to my plan.*

As she worked rapidly she felt the most creative that she had in quite some time. By late afternoon she began wrapping up her last project for the day. Sitting at her desk she heard someone speaking in deep accents that reverberated down the hall. "Recognize the voice?" the masculine tones inquired.

Startled, she looked up from her desk and glanced toward the door, her mind whirling as she asked, "Rick?"

A moment later he strolled into her office and sat down quickly in a chair across from her desk. Nervously his gaze met hers, awaiting a reaction. His dark eyes and deep voice, along with his subtle grin, always made her smile.

"What are you doing here?" she asked curiously, remaining seated at her desk. She felt too self-conscious to stand up in front of him.

"I was passing through and wanted to see you. I've been wondering how you're doing—how you're feeling." A pain echoed in his words and his eyes were moist. "I'm sorry I haven't called for a while."

Karen was unsure how to respond. *You should be sorry.* Instantly she bit her tongue.

"Sandy told me what's been going on with your health. Are you all right?" he asked, nervously glancing at the doorway.

"I'm on medication, and it seems to be helping. I just have to take it easy." *Like you care.*

"So you're going to be fine?" he repeated, searching for reassurance.

"Yes." She longed to believe that he really was concerned.

Slowly he arose from his chair and walked toward her. "I can't stay, but wanted to stop and check on you." On impulse she got up and walked around the desk, and the two embraced. Suddenly it was evident how much Karen's stomach had grown, for it got in the way of their hug. Startled, he released his grip quickly and fought the tears as the realization of her pregnancy overwhelmed him.

"I'm glad you stopped by," she said, attempting to break the tension.

"Me too." His voice broke. "Take care," he added, then fled out the door.

Stunned at what had just happened, she sat in the stillness of her office. It had been weeks since she had spoken to Rick, and months since she had seen him. Now he was gone again within minutes, leaving her emotionally frustrated and fragile once again. *How does he do this to me?* She was relieved that it was the end of the day, and that she could go home and sort through her thoughts and feelings. *I need to get away—soon.*

The phone was ringing as she walked through the door of her apartment 20 minutes later. "Hello," she said as she kicked off her shoes.

"Hi, Karen, it's Kathleen."

"Oh, hi, how's it going?" she asked, curiosity and anxiety mingling together.

"I have some exciting news for you. We've found adoptive parents for your baby!"

More emotions joined the mix. "Oh? Tell me about them." *Am I happy? Am I sad?*

"Their names are Andy and Abby, and they live in Tennessee," Kathleen began. "They are in their early thirties and have not been able to have children. Christians, they are very active in their church. He works in the music industry, and she is a part-time nurse, although she won't work at all once the baby is born. And both are musical."

Relief engulfed Karen. "They sound wonderful." *They really do sound perfect,* she thought. *Better parents than I would be. But . . .* She tried to shut off the feelings of jealousy rising within her.

"Yes, I thought you'd be pleased."

"Wow, I can't believe you found them so fast!" Karen was in shock.

"There are a lot of people wanting to adopt healthy Caucasian newborns," the woman reminded her.

"So what now?" *Yes, what now? What do I do?*

"Well, they've already been screened, so that's taken care of. The next step is finalizing the terms of the adoption agreement," Kathleen paused momentarily. "You and I have discussed the variety of options and gotten pretty specific about what you want in the agreement. Basically, we need just to get those down on paper and off to the attorney."

Karen thought quickly. "Is the couple agreeable to having a semi-open adoption? You know, to provide the agency with written updates and a photo every six months, so they are there if I want to see them?" *Will I want to?* She wasn't sure. *I need to leave that door open though . . .*

"Yes, they are willing."

"What do they think about the option for she and I to meet—once she turns 16?" Karen asked hesitantly. "After spending time with a student I know who was adopted, I've gained some insight of the adopted child's perspective. I believe that this is important to all of us."

"They agree and think that 16 is a good age—that she'd be old enough to be able to make that kind of choice in a responsible way."

"OK. Sounds like we're all in agreement then." Karen's stomach flip-flopped at the thought of not seeing her daughter for 16 years and then meeting her again!

"Yes, I think it's a good match," the woman summarized. "By the way, do you want to meet Andy and Abby before the baby is born? They are willing, if you are."

Karen tried to wrap her mind around that question. "I don't know," she began hesitantly. I hadn't given it any thought." *It's all happening too fast. Am I really ready for all this?*

Sensing Karen's dilemma, Kathleen said, "You don't have to decide now. It is just something that you might want to consider. Either way, Andy and Abby are fine with it."

"I'll think about it," Karen replied, lost in a whirlwind of thoughts.

"However," the woman from the adoption agency continued, "you do need to read through the information that we sent you concerning legal procedures and policy for when you are admitted to the hospital."

"Yes, I've already read through the package," Karen said, happy to discuss something less emotional. "It all makes sense. I've been working on a pseudonym that I can use." She felt like an undercover FBI agent or secret agent.

"Well, you have plenty of time, so there's no rush. But it's important to get familiar with the way everything works. All of the bills will be handled through the adoption agency, so you don't have to worry about a thing. Once you get to Nashville and preregister at the hospital, we will fax all the information to them. You don't have to handle any of those details yourself."

As Karen hung up the phone, she breathed a sigh of relief. *Thank You, Lord, for working things out once again.* Despite the obstacles along the way, the plan was coming together, step by step. *Now just give me strength to let her go!*

WEEK 31

Another tidal wave of pain engulfed her as she lay in bed, staring at her alarm clock. It was 5:15, way too early to be awake. After tossing and turning for almost an hour, attempting to find a comfortable position, she got up and headed for the shower, hoping that the hot water would help her relax. Pulsating on her shoulders and back, it did feel good, but it didn't take away the pain that overwhelmed her body every so often. *I thought the new medication was really working,* Karen thought to herself. *I need to call the doctor as soon as his office opens.*

After drying off and putting on her fluffy pink robe, she lumbered toward the kitchen for some hot chocolate. Her belly was large, and it was getting more and more difficult not to waddle. She didn't dare let her guard down, even in the privacy of her own home, for fear that she would do it in public.

As she put a cup of water into the microwave, she began to panic. *If I tell Dr. Jacobson about these pains, he's not going to let me travel to Nashville in a couple weeks,* she thought as she removed the steaming mug and tore open the packet of hot chocolate mix. *Maybe I shouldn't tell him . . . Nothing's going to keep me from going. Nothing!* she vowed. She had not made all those plans for nothing.

Her mind whirled like the contents of the mug she stirred. However, she snapped back to reality as she felt a warm sensation trickling down her legs. Puzzled, it took a few seconds for her to realize that her water had broken. She began to cry as she realized that there was no turning back now. At least she had made it to 31 weeks. *What should I do?* She panicked. *I'm all alone!*

For a long time she had known that Rick wouldn't be with her during the labor and delivery. Already aware what his answer would be, she hadn't asked him. He'd given her no support at all throughout her pregnancy, and she knew he wasn't about to start now. *Guess you never planned on always being there for me, no matter what.* She felt herself getting angry at him once again, the same emotion she had felt almost continually since she had first told him about her condition. Forcing the bitter thoughts aside, she told herself, *Concentrate, Karen. What am I going to do?*

Sandy was six hours away and was probably on her way to work. Karen decided against phoning her since she wouldn't be able to get away on such sort notice. *I've gotta do something.*

Sitting on the edge of a wooden chair in the kitchen, her legs and robe drenched, Karen put her elbows on the table, resting her head in her hands, and closed her eyes. *This isn't the way it's supposed to happen!* she sobbed. Picturing a large hospital in Nashville and Sandy there to support her, she cried. "Dear God, why?" she asked aloud. "I can't do this alone. I don't have the strength. Why are You letting this happen?"

Glancing at her watch, she began to time her contractions, the occasional tear still trickling down her cheek. Horrified, she discovered that they were five minutes apart. *I must get dressed and get to the hospital,* she thought as another wave of panic swept over her. *Oh! How can I do this alone?*

Which hospital should I go to? she wondered as she put on her maternity jeans. Dr. Jacobson was on staff at the nearby hospital, but not at the one in the city. She wanted her doctor now, not some stranger that she'd never even met. Yet Karen also knew that a premature baby would need all the latest technology that a city hospital could offer. *I'll call the office in a few minutes and ask where to go,* she concluded as she pulled her navy sweater over her head.

"Why today?" she asked God as she looked at her pale face in the mirror while combing her hair. The following day was her appointment with the OB/GYN in the city. *If I had already met her, I'd be more comfortable going to that hospital today.*

Desperately needing someone to talk to, she picked up the phone and dialed Rick's cell phone number, having waiting until one contraction was subsiding before calling, allowing herself five minutes to speak without being in pain. When he answered she acted cheerful and playfully chided, "Hey, let's swap jobs for the day."

He joked briefly then grew quiet, "So what are your plans?"

"My water broke a little while ago, so I guess you can imagine what my plans are."

Stunned, he eventually mumbled, "Are you OK? I mean, will you be all right since it's so early? I just saw you a few days ago," he stuttered, "and you seemed fine."

"I'm OK. But I've gotta go now." She knew the contractions would begin again soon.

"I'll pray for you. Call me back and let me know when it's over."

Somehow his promise to pray comforted her. Even through all of the stress and emotional pain of the past few months they had still prayed together many times. Early on in the pregnancy the prayers were selfish, as each of them begged God for a miscarriage. But later their prayers together were for forgiveness, for strength, and for peace. Still, she wished he had told her he was coming, that he would be at the hospital to hold her hand and help her through the ordeal.

Her next call was to work to let the secretary know that she wouldn't be in today. *What can I use for an excuse?* she thought before dialing. She had "been sick" several times during the past few weeks and knew that she needed something a little more original this time. *Since the students and teachers had begun a short vacation today, and most everyone would be gone for a few days, perhaps I'll just say that I will be working at home on a project both today and tomorrow.* Karen smiled to herself. That would buy her a couple days—Thursday and Friday—plus she'd also have the weekend. A few minutes later, in between contractions, Karen phoned in. After hanging up, she sighed heavily, relieved that no one had questioned her actions or her excuse. *One less thing to worry about.*

Next she telephoned Dr. Jacobson's office. After Karen explained that her water had broken and that she was in active labor, the nurse instructed her to have someone drive her immediately to the hospital in the city, almost an hour away.

Frustrated, Karen hung up and faced the reality that she didn't have anyone to help her. *I'm alone. There is nobody but me.* As she walked through her apartment, tears streaming down her cheeks, she angrily slammed the bedroom door and kicked the couch. *This isn't how it was supposed to happen!* Then, managing to regain her composure, she threw a few items into her overnight bag and stumbled to the car.

Another wave of pain hit as she turned the ignition key. Gripping the leather-covered steering wheel, she closed her eyes and began breathing through the contraction. *I hope no one walks through the parking lot and notices me leaning over the steering wheel,* she thought halfway through the contraction. But the pain was so intense that she didn't care what happened.

When the pain subsided Karen leaned back in the seat and shifted the car into gear. However, the contractions were coming frequently and growing in intensity, causing her to keep pulling off the road. *"God, why do I have to do this alone?"* Her heart ached. Why had Rick let her down when she needed him the most?

After several stops within the first 10 miles she decided to drive to Dr. Jacobson's office, which was located across from the small community hospital, instead of trying to make it to the city. The pain had become too difficult to manage by herself.

Arriving at the two-story brick professional building just before 9:00, she stumbled painfully through the front door. Another contraction consumed her, and Karen propped herself up against a wall, halfway down the carpeted hallway. *Breathe! Breathe!* she reminded herself, wanting to pass out.

Once inside the office, the receptionist took one look at her and ran down the hall to locate the nurse. Quickly guided to an exam room, the doctor checked her and with a concerned expression on his face explained that she was fully dilated and that the birth would be soon. Urgently, he instructed the nurse to take her in a wheelchair across to the hospital and straight to the delivery room.

As the elevator doors opened onto the fourth floor, and the office nurse pushed her toward the birthing center, Karen was only partially coherent. Everything was a blur as the woman whisked her through the double wooden doors and into a private suite.

A petite dark-haired nurse rushed into the room behind them. "I'll take her from here," she said to the office nurse as she assisted Karen out of the wheelchair and onto the bed.

"Good luck, Karen," the nurse from Dr. Jacobson's office offered as she left the room, pushing the wheelchair.

"My name is Meg. Let's get you changed," the hospital nurse said as she held out the flimsy blue and white gown. "I'll help you with that sweater."

It was a struggle even to get undressed, for every two minutes a contraction would halt the process. "Breathe!" the nurse coached as Karen sat on the bed, cringing in agony.

After Karen finished changing she lay in bed, propped up by several pillows while Meg took her vital signs. "Will your husband be arriving soon?" the nurse asked as she checked her blood pressure.

For a moment Karen hesitated. "I'm not married," she replied, unsure about how to share the rest. "And I'm placing the baby for adoption," she explained, avoiding Meg's eyes and staring at the bed. *I'm giving her up . . .* The words hit her. Sweetie would no longer be a part of her life.

When she finally had the courage to look up she noticed that the nurse's eyes were moist. Meg reached over and squeezed her hand, coaching her through the next contraction. "You can do it. Breathe! Breathe!"

Karen gripped the nurse's hand back with all her might. The urge to push overrode everything. "Where's the doctor?" she screamed. "I've got to push!"

As if on cue, Dr. Jacobson hurried into the room, dressed from head to toe in dark-blue scrubs. "How are you doing, Karen?" he asked as he checked her with a gloved hand.

Without giving her a chance to respond he barked out commands to the nearby nurses. "Break the bed down for delivery—the baby's crowning. Bring the sterile cart over here and the lights."

By the time the next contraction began everything was in place and Dr. Jacobson gave Karen the OK to push. It only took two pushes until Karen heard the cries of her baby.

The infant's cries were sporadic, almost a whimper, and not nearly as strong as she remembered Sarah's at her birth. Karen's heart jumped. She could tell the baby was struggling. *Please let my baby be OK!* she begged God as tears streamed down her face. *God, don't let her die!*

Stunned, she watched as the nurse carried her tiny, wrinkled, dark-haired baby through the doors and out to the life-flight helicopter to transfer her to a larger city that had a neonatal unit. Karen had chosen not to hold her, for she knew that she could never let her go if she did. *Goodbye, Sweetie,* she whispered silently. *I love you.*

Karen had given birth one hour after arriving at the hospital. As is typical with premature births, labor had been fast—only five hours—and for that she was grateful.

Back in the birthing suite the nurses were unusually quiet as they went about their duties, seemingly at a loss for what to say to a woman who was placing her newborn for adoption. In such a small town adoptions were rare.

Eventually, someone from patient registration located her, and she checked in under an assumed name as the adoption agency had instructed her. Soon the hospital transferred her to a private room on another floor so that she could avoid seeing babies or hear them cry. Her new room was sterile and small, all white, and much different than the suites in the birthing center.

As she lay on the firm mattress, trying to get comfortable and attempting to process her thoughts and feelings, Dr. Jacobson entered the room and sat on the edge of the bed, placing his hand on hers. "I think your baby's going to be OK," he began confidently. "She weighed a little more than four pounds and has a fighting spirit. Once she gets to the neonatal unit in the city she'll stabilize and will be well taken care of."

Karen smiled as she wiped away tears. Both she and Rick were fighters. "I was worried when it took so much effort for her to breath and cry."

"Try to get some rest. I'll check on you again this evening," Dr. Jacobson said as he squeezed her hand and then left the room.

Within minutes Meg arrived, peeking into the room quietly to see if Karen was sleeping before walking in. "I wanted to check on you. How are you?" she asked as she stood beside the bed, searching Karen's bloodshot eyes for answers.

"I must be in shock or something since all I can do is cry." Then again, that was nothing she wasn't accustomed to. *The past six and a half months have been nothing but tears,* she thought wryly.

"That's normal right now. Do you need any help making phone calls? Have you contacted anyone yet?"

Karen froze. "Oh!" Reaching for her purse, she pulled out Kathleen's business card and passed it to Meg. "Would you call this woman and tell her where they took the baby?"

"Of course." The nurse hurried out of the room.

Wanting to sit up instead of lie down, Karen propped her pillows higher. As her thoughts turned to her baby, she instinctively put her hands on her stomach, only to feel flabby skin. Tears welled again, and Karen could not stop shaking and crying as the loss overwhelmed her. *You're gone forever now, Sweetie. I'll never hold you.* Her pain seemed unbearable.

She was also becoming obsessed with leaving the hospital. *What is the point in staying?* her thoughts went round and round. *I can heal at home as well as I can here. And I don't want all this attention.* After fighting the urge to go home for almost two hours, Karen finally gave in to it.

When the nurse came to do her vital signs, Karen said matter of factly, "I want you to call my doctor and tell him that I am getting dressed and checking myself out."

The nurse wasted no time in getting Dr. Jacobson on the telephone. "Karen, please reconsider this," he begged. "You need to stay for a while to make sure that you're OK."

"The reason that mothers stay in the hospital after delivery is for the babies," she replied, "to make sure they don't get jaundice or whatever. Since my baby isn't here, there's no reason for me to stay." She choked back tears. "I can't stand it here! I just can't!"

"Since this is not your first experience giving birth, I won't stop you. However, you must promise to telephone my office at the end of the day, just to check in."

After signing a large stack of papers, she called a cab to drive her home. She would pick up her car in a day or two when she was feeling better.

Sore and exhausted, Karen shuffled into her apartment. The doctor had prescribed medication to help her relax, and she swallowed a pill with a glass of water before heading for the couch. Its familiar green and burgundy fabric comforted her.

Before she would allow herself to sleep, however, she telephoned Rick to update him, as she had promised.

"Hello."

"Hi, there," she said softly.

"How are things going?" he asked in a frightened tone.

"I'm OK." Karen felt the medicine kicking in already. "It's over. She was born a little after 10:00 this morning."

After a lengthy pause he said, "I'm glad you're OK. How long do you have to stay in the hospital?"

"I checked myself out—I couldn't stand to be there." Her speech got slower and slower as the medicine began to take effect.

"Are you sure that's wise? I don't want anything to happen to you."

"I'm going to sleep now. Call me tonight, would you?" Soon she drifted off.

Between dozing, she spent every waking moment thinking about her child. She felt lost without her baby kicking to let her know that she was all right. Wondering what hospital they had flown her to, she tried to imagine what the neonatal nursery looked like, picturing one that she had seen on a television program several years before. The bassinets were glass and sterile. Tiny little bodies lay with all kinds of wires and catheters protruding awkwardly from their bodies. Karen cried until she shook, unable to get the horrible images out of her mind.

I hope that Kathleen and the adoptive parents are with her right now, she thought before falling asleep again.

At times when she awoke she felt waves of tremendous relief, knowing that it was over. There would be no more hiding, no more pretending, and no more plans to make for her future. She had made it through successfully, although not unscathed. The counselor from the adoption agency had warned her that she would still have to endure a tremendous amount of emotional trauma once the delivery was over. *I don't want to even think about it right now. I'm too exhausted. Later. Much later.* Karen faded away into sleep again. At least when she was sleeping she wasn't crying or thinking about her child.

Fortunately most of Karen's coworkers were away on a break, which made her absence less noticeable. Undisturbed, she spent the remainder of the day resting.

That evening when Rick called again, she shared with him some thoughts that she had had. "You know, Rick, I'm convinced that if I had delivered in the city hospital, and the baby had remained in the neonatal unit at the same hospital that I was in, I would probably not have been able to go through with the adoption." Her voice broke. "If I had seen her in the nursery," she sniffled, "so tiny and fragile . . ." She struggled to hold back the floodgates. "I never would have been able to give her up. I would have spent every last second in the nursery with her, falling more in love with her by the minute."

THREE DAYS AFTER DELIVERY

Karen lay in bed Sunday morning, stalling, not wanting to get up. Although the sun filtered through the unopened mini blinds, indicating a beautiful spring day outside, she still felt disoriented, in a daze from the events of the past few days. She glanced at her small alarm clock on the nightstand and was surprised that it was already after 10:00. Usually she was not one to sleep in late. Lately, however, all she had wanted to do was sleep. As she tried to coax herself into getting up, the phone rang.

"Hello," she mumbled, sitting up in the large bed as she spoke.

"Hi, Karen, it's Kathleen. How are you doing?"

"I'm OK, I guess," she began halfheartedly, grateful that she didn't have to sound too convincing. "I'm still trying to process everything that's happened." *It all seems like a bad dream.*

"That's normal. Just rest as much as you can, and you'll start to feel better soon."

"I hope so."

"I've been at the hospital with Andy and Abby, and I wanted to update you on how the baby's doing."

Karen's heart leapt. "How is she?" she asked cautiously.

"She's OK. Lost a little weight, but apparently that's normal."

"What's wrong?" Karen interrupted. "How could that happen? She can't afford to lose weight—she was so small to begin with!"

"Calm down. Remember, preemies always take extra care, but the doctor said she'll be fine."

"All right." Karen's voice broke.

"Andy and Abby are wonderful, Karen. They love her so much. They haven't left the hospital since she arrived."

"Kathleen." Karen pulled herself together. "I keep having this thought about her—about Sweetie. It's so persistent—it just won't go away."

"What is it?"

"I want you to talk with the doctor and ask him to play music for her in her bassinette, or whatever they call those things. I'm convinced that music will help her thrive, to get stronger faster. This thought keeps running through my head, and I can't shake it." She shared with the woman from the adoption agency how important music was to her and Rick, and how she believed that their child had been born with that same love for music. "Please talk with the doctor soon, Kathleen. Do it for me, would you?"

"Of course. I'll speak to him today."

"Thanks. Keep me posted, would you?"

"Of course I will. Karen, what are your plans for the next week or two? Have you given any thought about how to get back into a daily routine?"

"I need to just to take my mind off everything. I was lucky that I went into labor during the short vacation that the school had, so no one really missed me while I was out. But classes resume tomorrow, and I need to get back to work for at least part of the day."

"That's a bit soon, don't you think?"

"Maybe. But I need to keep busy. Laying around all day is driving me crazy!"

"What does your doctor say?"

"We haven't spoken about it. I'm stubborn, so he knows I'm going to do what I want to do anyway."

"Yes, you are." The woman chuckled. "But seriously, Karen, take it easy. Don't overdo it and harm yourself."

"When I get tired, I'll come home," Karen promised.

"OK. I'll phone you again in a couple weeks. In the meantime, Dr. Dawn Evans, the psychologist from the agency, will call to check on you and provide counseling. OK?"

"Sure. We spoke several times before the baby was born."

After hanging up, Karen made her way slowly to the shower. Still sore from giving birth, she hoped that the hot water would not only soothe her physical pain, but also the emotional. The water felt relaxing as it pulsated against her back. Standing there for what seemed like an hour, she finally had to force herself to twist the chrome knob and face the day.

What should I do? Karen asked herself as she finished pulling on her maternity jeans and sweater. The jeans were baggy, but she knew her regular jeans wouldn't fit yet—she still had weight to lose and flabby skin to tone up.

I've got to get out of the house, just for a little while. Maybe I'll go to the bookstore in the mall and look for something to read, to keep my mind occupied. She smiled as she pictured herself relaxing on the couch, engrossed in a thick book. More motivated now, she threw on a windbreaker as she headed slowly out the door.

The mall was quiet, and Karen was pleased not to have to fight crowds. As she entered the large bookstore, the smell of new books permeated the air. She loved to read, but always seemed to be too busy to spend as much time as she would like with a book. Roaming the aisles, her eyes drank in the many titles as she searched for just the right book.

About 20 minutes later she rounded a book stack and came face-to-face with a blond-haired, petite woman standing in the next aisle, fumbling with a book with one hand while trying to cradle a newborn baby with the other. Startled, Karen froze in her tracks, the dark-haired infant directly in front of her. The child was wrapped in a soft pink blanket, and her eyes fluttered, as if trying to open. A few seconds later she made a soft crying sound.

Panicked, Karen turned and hurried toward the door, trying not to break down completely until she was outside the store. As she sat by the waterfall in the center court of the massive glass and stone mall, Karen stared at the water, hoping that no one would see her tears. She cried quietly, the pain flooding over her. *How will I ever get over this?* she wondered as she wiped her eyes. *I miss her so much. Am I going to have this kind of reaction every time I see a newborn baby? Is it going to tear my heart out each time? Dr. Evans says this will get easier over time, but I don't see how! I miss you, Sweetie. I miss you.*

Karen spent the remainder of the day watching television, dozing off and on and longing to escape the pain of her heartbreak.

Startled by the telephone out of one of her naps, she sat up on the couch. "Hello."

"Hi, Karen," Sandy greeted, although not sounding like her usual self. "How are you feeling?"

"Kinda rough at the moment. This is going to take a long time to get over—if ever."

"I'm so sorry." Sandy's voice faltered, and Karen could tell that she was also on the verge of tears. "I can't imagine what you're going through." She sniffled.

"You sound kind of rough, yourself. Are you OK?"

"I feel pretty low, although I'm not sure why," Sandy confessed, still sniffling. "I'm sorry I couldn't make it up to see you, but this is a hectic time at school, and I can't get away."

"I understand." She knew that Sandy's job and two children kept her extremely busy.

"Maybe in a few weeks I can take a long weekend and drive up."

"That's fine. And maybe I'll feel more like company by that time. Right now all I do is sleep." Truthfully, Karen wasn't up to having anyone around.

"Take care, Karen. I must go now."

"Thanks for checking on me. But don't worry—I'll be OK. Bye." *I wish I believed that.* Karen wondered if she'd ever feel fine again. The counselor that telephoned her each day had promised that she would—in time. But she had so much to work through in the meantime.

THREE WEEKS AFTER DELIVERY

Slowly Karen managed to get back into a regular routine as she resumed her duties at school, grateful for the diversion that work provided. It was her escape, something to focus on other than Sweetie. She threw herself even deeper into what would have normally been run-of-the-mill projects. *I'll get through this,* she told herself fiercely. *I'm a fighter.*

Nighttime was the hardest, and she dreaded climbing into bed each evening. Talking to her unborn child before falling asleep had become a habit, and now she was alone. Finally, she had started praying for Sweetie each night at the same time, attempting to fill the void.

The phone was ringing as Karen walked through the door that Tuesday evening after work. "Hello," she answered, out of breath from rushing.

"Hi, Karen, how's it going?" Sandy asked in a subdued tone.

Wow! She sounds very down tonight, Karen thought, slumping onto the couch. "Hi there," she said aloud as she kicked her shoes off and pulled her legs up beside her. "Sounds like I should ask how you are tonight!"

"I'm OK," Sandy began halfheartedly. "I was thinking of you and hadn't called you in a few days, so I thought I'd check in."

"Each day gets a little better. I've been working hard at staying busy, keeping my mind occupied, and that's the only way that I'm surviving. So what's got you down tonight?" she pressed.

"Honestly, Karen, I think I'm having a hard time with this whole situation also," her friend began, sniffling as she spoke. "I became attached to the baby, because of you and Rick, and I realized this week that it's having an impact on me . . . on my emotions."

Tears streamed down Karen's cheeks as the realization of what Sandy had just said hit her between the eyes. She had been so wrapped up in her own life and her own pain that she hadn't even considered the emotional toll that it might be taking on Sandy. Both women wept, lost in their own thoughts.

Finally, Karen regained enough composure to say something. "I'm so sorry, Sandy. I didn't want to hurt you. I never stopped to think what this might do to you." Her mind wandered as she spoke. "Perhaps I shouldn't have told you and gotten you involved."

"No, Karen. I wouldn't have wanted that. I'll be OK in time, just as you will. It's taken a while to figure out why I've been so low, but now that I understand, it's a little easier to deal with."

"I'm sorry," Karen repeated as she wiped her eyes. *I never could have guessed how much pain this has caused everyone.*

"So, have you heard from Rick?" Sandy changed the subject.

"He called a couple times that first week to check on me. But I've not heard a word since then." Pain arose in her chest, as it did each time her thoughts returned to him.

"Does that mean that your relationship is over?" Sandy asked hesitantly.

"Yes," Karen admitted. *It had died a long time ago.*

"Then I guess you're working through two losses instead of one. That must be terrible."

"If it wasn't for counseling, I don't know what'd I'd do."

"Well keep doing it. Maybe I'll go for a few sessions myself."

"You should."

"I should get busy, Karen, but I wanted to see how you're doing."

"You too. Bye."

A few days later Kathleen called again. "How's she doing?" Karen asked nervously.

"You wouldn't believe it!" the woman bubbled. "She's gained weight. The doctor's says she's doing better than they anticipated . . . and that she'll be going home in a couple days."

"Wonderful! Did they play music to her?" Tears of joy filled Karen's eyes.

"Yes, continually."

"That's good news!" A weight lifted from her chest.

"So how are you holding up? Has Dr. Evans been calling you regularly?"

"Yes, we talk often, and it helps a lot."

"Great. She will continue working with you until she is comfortable about your emotional progress."

"OK."

"Well, I thought I'd update you on the baby's progress."

"Thanks for calling. I'm very relieved." Karen felt a peace fill her heart. Her baby was fine. They would both make it.

THREE MONTHS AFTER DELIVERY

Summer had arrived. Although she had to work during it, unlike many of the teachers, things went at a more leisurely pace.

It was a Tuesday afternoon, and Karen was spending her lunch hour by a nearby waterfall, relaxing in a lounge chair in shorts and tank top, drinking in the rays of the sun. She had lost the weight she had gained while pregnant and had also discovered, much to her delight, that because of her improved diet while pregnant, she had also gone down an entire dress size.

As she lay in the lounge, eyes closed and legs and arms outstretched, her mind wrestled with the impending picnic that she had been invited to attend that evening. The school staff had a tradition of getting together to commemorate the conclusion of another school year.

Fear pounded in her chest as she thought about who would be at the picnic. *I don't want to go. I can't handle being around babies.* The host this year and his wife had just had a baby a few weeks earlier. Additionally, there would be about 30 other guests, and she knew that at least one of the families had also recently had a baby.

Maybe I should call at the last minute and bow out, saying that I'm sick. The idea sent a surge of relief through her. However, as she wrestled with the realization that she was letting fear control her life and her actions, she became angry with herself. *What am I going to do?* she asked herself as she folded up her chair, placed it in the trunk of her car, and headed back to work.

The rest of the afternoon she struggled with whether or not to attend the picnic. Her thoughts vacillated back and forth. One minute she was determined to go, not to let her fears win out. The next she was petrified, ready to run in the opposite direction.

By late afternoon Karen decided that she would skip the picnic and go to the mall as a diversion. *Why push it? I'm not going to heal emotionally from this in an instant. I can work on it again tomorrow. But for now I deserve a break.*

Yet as she drove toward the mall, she felt disgusted with herself. "This is so stupid!" she exclaimed aloud. "I can't run and hide forever. I'm going to face this situation—this fear—head-on."

Once she turned the car around, though, she realized there was no re-treating now. The closer she got to the picnic site, the more ferociously her heart beat in her chest. *What if I break down in front of everybody? What if . . . ?* Suddenly she remembered that her friends' house was large and had a spacious yard, so she would have plenty of room to keep her distance from the babies. *I'll do this, and I'll succeed.*

After parking her car and inhaling deeply, she walked slowly toward some of the guests mingling in the side yard. Spotting Emily, she smiled.

"Hi, Karen. I was wondering if you were coming. Usually you're the first one to arrive at these gatherings."

"I know. I'm just not my usual self right now. Got a minute to talk?"

"Sure." Emily looked questioningly at her as they made their way to a quiet corner of the yard. "Are you going to finally tell me what's been wrong with you?"

Karen wasn't ready to share the whole story, and she wasn't sure if she ever would be. "Rick and I have broken up." Her eyes were moist as she said the words aloud. "We haven't been getting along for quite some time, and it's over."

Emily hugged her tightly. "I'm sorry. I know you loved him." Karen was thankful that her friend did not comment further. She already knew the younger woman's opinion of Rick, and she wasn't quite ready to admit that maybe Emily had been right.

Feeling herself on the verge of tears, Karen glanced around and changed the subject quickly. "Isn't this a great place? The house is beauti-ful, the yard is huge, and what a gorgeous pool!"

"Yes, Dan and Betty are blessed." They walked back toward the rest of the group. "Have you seen their new baby? He's adorable."

"Uh, no, I haven't seen him yet," Karen stuttered.

Emily laughed. "He's the happiest baby you'll ever see! Hey, I need to go find Grant and my kids. He took them for a walk, and I'm not sure where they ended up. I'll catch up to you later." She headed toward an old gray barn that sat adjacent to the property line.

Karen spoke to several other staff members on the way to the house— to face Betty and her newborn son. *I'm going to look at him and force myself to be around him for just as long as I can stand it. That's the only way I'm going to work through this.*

She paused at the large oak door, her hand on the brass knob. Then breathing deeply, she twisted and pushed. Unexpectedly she came face to face with Betty, on her way out to mingle with the guests. In her arms she held the baby, dressed in a blue and white sleeper and sound asleep. Nervous perspiration trickled down Karen's forehead and into her eyes. Speechless, she stood, poised in mid-step.

"Hi, Karen." Betty greeted her with a smile. "Glad you could come over."

"Thank you." She scrambled for words. Soon two other guests caught up with Betty and began talking, doting over the baby. Karen welcomed the opportunity to slip away quietly. Tears welled in the corners of her eyes, but she fought to keep them at bay. *I won't give in! I'm going to be strong and get through this.*

Several times during the next two hours Karen spoke to Betty, forcing herself to stand close to the baby and to look at him. Each time got easier and the close proximity a little less stressful.

On the drive home that evening Karen glanced at the sun sinking below the distant trees and casting its golden glow across the hillsides. She replayed the day, glad that she had not let her fear hold her captive. Each day was a little easier, a little less painful.

That evening she picked up the phone and called Dr. Evans for their weekly counseling session. She needed to talk about her day.

"Hi, Karen, how are you?" Dr. Evans said, upbeat as usual.

"It's been a difficult day." She went on to describe all that had happened, eager to hear her reaction to what had happened.

"Sounds as if you made the right choice. I'm glad you went to the picnic and dealt with it," the psychologist commented. "If you keep doing those kinds of things you'll work through the initial 'shell-shock,' as I call it, and you'll be able to function again within social situations."

The women also chatted about Karen's impending decision about viewing the update and photo of the baby. As per the legal agreement, the adoptive parents had to report to the adoption agency every six months. Karen could either have them sent on to her or have them held at the agency until a later date. "Are you ready to take that next step?" Evans asked cautiously.

"I've been thinking about it . . ." Her voice stumbled.

"That clause was something that you requested," the woman reminded.

"Yes, I know. But I don't know if I'll be ready by then or if I'll wait a little longer," Karen answered after a moment.

"You have three more months to decide, so don't worry about it now.

"You know, Karen, I'm a Christian. And as I talk with you and get to know your situation, I am profoundly reminded about how great God is. I think we all have preconceptions of Him—about how He reacts to our mistakes and to our problems. It's easy for us to assume that He has the same outcome planned for all women who face unplanned pregnancy. Yet through your circumstance I have seen that He's not locked inside a box— that He's not required to operate the way that we think He should. He has so many ways to take care of us . . . to see us through . . . to solve our problems . . . and we can't even begin to count the ways."

SIX MONTHS AFTER DELIVERY

Karen's life had returned to a normal rhythm. Her work was still a high priority, a means of affirmation and a way to keep her mind occupied. And her weekly counseling sessions with Dr. Evans had turned into bi-weekly, eventually progressing to "call if you need me."

Because the psychologist no longer phoned regularly, her call one afternoon caught Karen by surprise. "Hi, Karen, this is Dr. Evans," a cheerful voice greeted her.

"Oh, hi." *What's going on?*

"I just wanted to let you know that the update arrived from Andy and Abby today. Are you ready to have me mail it to you?"

Karen slumped onto the couch. Although she knew this day was coming, it still knocked the wind out of her. "What do you think I should do?" she asked in a nervous, breathless voice.

"You're the one that must make the decision, Karen, not me."

"I know. I've thought about it so many times." She took a deep breath before continuing. "Yes. The answer is yes. Please send it to me."

"OK, I'll get it right out."

After hanging up, Karen sat on the couch, lost in thought. Her hands were sweaty, and she still found it hard to breathe.

Am I really ready for this? she asked herself as she lay down on the couch, propping a small pillow beneath her head. Her thoughts were chaotic.

What am I afraid of? I've seen her face in the dreams. I wonder if she'll look the same? She smiled at the thought.

What am I really afraid of? Karen asked herself a second time.

Maybe I'm afraid of becoming too attached again . . . Tears flowed as she remembered the intense emotional pain during the weeks that followed the birth. The loss had been overwhelming. She had cried and cried and at times had been convinced that the pain would kill her. Time had helped to ease that pain—to make it more manageable—but it was a slow process.

What if reading the update and seeing her picture slams me back to that point again emotionally? I'm not ready for such pain again.

During the next couple days Karen nervously anticipated the arrival of the package. Each day she checked her mailbox, holding her breath as she glanced through the mail, always relieved not to find anything from the adoption agency. But at the same time her nervousness grew as she knew that the next day would most likely be "the day."

Three days later the package finally appeared. As she stood in her apartment, holding the manila envelope, her heart pounded. This was it. She was about to come face-to-face with her daughter. *Will she resemble me or look more like her dad?* Her hand shook as she gripped the envelope tightly.

Do I really want to do this? she asked herself once again. *I don't have to open it. I can put it away until another day.* She toyed with the idea, but knew down deep that she was ready to take that next step.

Slowly, methodically, she turned the envelope over and slid her finger beneath the sealed tab. *This is it,* she thought, a hint of excitement replacing her nervousness as she opened the package.

EPILOGUE : THREE YEARS LATER

Karen couldn't wait to see Sandy. It had been almost two years since they had last visited, and now Karen's business trip to the east coast had put her within an hour of her friend's home. They had scheduled a lunch together to get caught up.

Once they had been close friends. But almost without acknowledging why, they'd slowly ceased contact. Weeks turned into months, and months had melted into two years. Neither had wanted their friendship to end— it was more related to the painful memories surrounding the emotional journey they had shared.

"Karen!" Sandy exclaimed as she stepped into the lobby. They embraced as if the two years had never existed.

As they sat down Karen wondered what the past couple years had been like for her friend. Sandy's life was predictable and stable, but Karen still hoped that some day a man would step into the picture and bring her friend joy and spontaneity.

Sandy shared how her life had remained on target in regard to her plans for the future. An inveterate planner, she always had both short-term and long-term goal lists at hand. Her career was progressing on schedule, and her children were succeeding in school.

Eventually Sandy changed the subject. "That's enough about me. Tell me how you really are doing," she begged.

"You know, time is an amazing blessing," Karen dabbed at her mouth with the linen napkin. "I'm very different than I was three years ago, and I'm grateful for that." She paused, choosing her words. "I still have painful moments—I probably always will. Yet, most of the time I'm happy and content, at peace about the decision that I made."

"Good." Sandy smiled.

"I enjoy my job. This new position is challenging, but I enjoy the variety. And I'm proud of Sarah—she's doing so well in college. What more could I want?"

"Do you ever hear from Rick?" Sandy inquired cautiously.

"No, and I'm glad. One day I woke up and realized that I didn't need him. I deserved to be treated much better than that."

"That's wonderful, Karen."

"The counseling has helped more than anything. It's been a crucial piece in my emotional recovery. I've not only worked through the loss of my baby daughter, but also that of Rick—and several other issues, as well." Karen caught her breath and smiled. "As I look to the future, and when I dream about dating, I know I'll be searching for a very different kind of man!"

Both women chuckled.

Reaching into her purse, Karen pulled out a burgundy envelope and handed it to Sandy. "Read this," Karen said, eyes brimming with emotion.

"What is it?" Cautiously Sandy held the worn envelope.

"It's a card from Abby and Andy that I received right after Mother's day this year," Karen said, choking up as she always did when she thought about it. "Each year around Mother's Day I get a card like this."

"Dear Karen:

"Every year as Mother's Day arrives I think of you, even more than usual.

"I think about the beautiful daughter you entrusted to us three years ago. I think about how painful that must have been for you, both physically and emotionally. She is growing steadily, and she's healthy and happy.

"I just want you to know that each year we love her more than the year before.

"Thank you,
"Abby & Andy"

Resources for Unplanned Pregnancy

Many agencies are ready and willing to assist you in making decisions regarding an unplanned pregnancy. I've listed only a few within this resource section, for lack of space. I'd love to hear from you. You can e-mail me at: thepromisebook@hotmail.com.

—Karen

Below is a list of typical ways in which agencies can provide help:
- ✔Completely confidential help
- ✔Free pregnancy testing
- ✔Non-judgmental and caring advice
- ✔Friendship and emotional support
- ✔Legal, medical, and educational referrals
- ✔Prenatal information
- ✔Maternity and baby clothes
- ✔Housing referrals
- ✔Social agency referrals
- ✔Information on other community services
- ✔ Adoption information

Adoption.com
www.crisispregnancy.com

America's Pregnancy Help Line
http://thehelpline.org
1-800-672-2296

Birthright International
www.birthright.org
1-800-550-4900

CPS Pregnancy Resources
www.cpcqc.org
1-309-797-3636

Also, look in your hometown phone book. Someone to talk with may be just a phone call and a few miles away!

Adoption Agencies and Information

Below are some of the benefits of adoption, courtesy of helpline.org:

Birthmother:
- ✔Housing assistance may be available
- ✔Counseling and support
- ✔The opportunity to fulfill your dreams whether educational, travel, or career
- ✔The opportunity to make the dreams you have for your child come true
- ✔Prenatal and delivery expenses paid as needed
- ✔A better choice of excellent doctors and staff
- ✔You get to choose a family for your child that you like best, and can get to know them personally
- ✔A support group of birth mothers who will share their experiences with you
- ✔Members of your family may also receive counseling/support services
- ✔All legal expenses and attorney fees will be paid for you
- ✔The opportunity to bring many people a lot of happiness that could not occur without you
- ✔The happiness that comes with knowing that the adoptive parents know you love this baby enough to ensure his or her happiness

Benefits for the Child:
- ✔The love and support of adoptive parents who are emotionally and financially ready to parent
- ✔The kind of home and family life that you desire for your child
- ✔A two parent home that may also include a brother or sister
- ✔Resources and provisions that might not otherwise be provided for financially
- ✔A greater probability of good education and going to college

Benefits for the Adoptive Family:
- ✔Receive the joy and blessing of adding a child to their family
- ✔Opportunity to go through the pregnancy and related experiences

that would not otherwise be possible
✔Ability to fulfill dreams of raising a child

Once again, we have listed only a few of the adoption agencies available. Hundreds more can be located by using search engines such as Google. However, when considering an agency, always make sure that the agency is licensed.

Bethany Christian Services
www.bethany.org
1-800-bethany

Lifetime Adoption Facilitation Center
www.lifetimeadoption.com
1-800-923-6784

A Child's Waiting
http://achildswaiting.com
1-866-yes-adopt